St. Joseph's Chapel, Ursuline Academy, Arcadia

*M*isouri's rural electric cooperatives and their official publication, *Rural Missouri*, are proud to present *Faith of Our Fathers: The Churches of Missouri*. This book was made possible by the many submissions from readers of *Rural Missouri* who share a special love for their churches.

When the first settlers arrived in Missouri, they brought their faith with them. Often it was this faith that brought them to the new world in the first place, because they were fleeing religious persecution in Europe. In Missouri they found an opportunity to build new communities, in most cases centered around the church.

In my years with *Rural Missouri* magazine, I have had the good fortune to worship in many rural churches. I have walked the woods in the Irish Wilderness where Father Hogan tried to start a community for Irish immigrants. I've seen the giant praying hands near Webb City and the many signs of faith—from cathedrals to back-yard shrines—that Missourians have built. It's fascinating to drive into a new town and to see it first by the magnificent spires that point toward the heavens.

When the first electric cooperatives were formed, they wasted no time in wiring the rural churches. Many interesting and even humorous stories came out of this effort. For example, linemen at Farmers' Electric tell how the co-op wired its churches without meters, giving them free electricity at first. This practice had to end when the co-op's thrifty homemakers used the free power to hold ironing bees in the church basement.

One of my favorite stories was told by C. Wendell Froshee of Willard, Missouri, in the book *The Day the Lights Came On*. His story tells how electricity first came to Rose Hill Baptist Church located five miles north of Willard and served by Ozark Electric Cooperative.

"We had the church wired and the church records state that we furnished the material and paid the man to wire it a total of $10. After it was completed, the church thought it would be nice to have a little ceremony. So the first Wednesday night after it was done we all gathered for prayer meeting at the usual time. The janitor had the lamps all trimmed and burning, at the proper time the oil lamps were put out and the switch turned on for the first time. Well you guessed it, nothing happened. We were all in the dark, the lamps were relit and a discussion followed. Finally one of our older men stood and addressed us and this is what he said: 'We shouldn't be alarmed because the electricity had to come all the way from Mt. Vernon, Missouri.' Being eight years old, that sounded good to me. However, some wiser minds checked things out and got it working."

Electricity meant a lot to those who received it for the first time, especially when the benefits of indoor plumbing were realized.

Missouri's electric cooperatives are proud to serve the state's many rural churches. Just as the church serves a vital role in the community, so too does the electric cooperative. It provides more than electricity, bringing jobs, essential services, and a new commitment to community to the countryside.

—Jim McCarty, Editor
Rural Missouri
May 2007

St. Genevieve Catholic Church, Ste. Genevieve

Faith of Our Fathers
The Churches of Missouri

BY
LINDA C. KERNS
FOR
Rural Missouri

THE
DONNING COMPANY
PUBLISHERS

St. John Lutheran Church, Schubert

The Donning Company Publishers
184 Business Park Drive, Suite 206
Virginia Beach, VA 23462

Steve Mull, General Manager
Barbara B. Buchanan, Office Manager
Richard A. Horwege, Senior Editor
Chris Daniel, Graphic Designer
Cindy Smith, Project Research Coordinator
Scott Rule, Director of Marketing
Tonya Hannink, Marketing Coordinator

Ed Williams, Project Director

Library of Congress Cataloging-in-Publication Data

Kerns, Linda C.
    Faith of our fathers : the churches of Missouri / by Linda C. Kerns for Rural Missouri.
        p. cm.
    Includes index.
    ISBN 978-1-57864-457-5 (hard cover : alk. paper)
1. Church buildings—Missouri. 2. Missouri—Church history. I. Rural Missouri 1995 (Project) II. Title.
    NA5230.M7K47 2007
    726.509778—dc22

                                                          2007034716

Printed in the USA by Walsworth Publishing Company

CONTENTS

A Word On This Book

Faith of Our Fathers is a follow-up to the highly successful *Barns of Missouri* published by *Rural Missouri*. As with the previous book, our goal was to preserve some of the landmarks that are rapidly vanishing from the Missouri landscape. In creating this book we regret that we were unable to include all of the churches in the state. We relied on readers of *Rural Missouri* to submit their churches, and were overwhelmed by the response. This book contains just a fraction of what was sent in. At best, this is a cross-section of church styles and faiths. We hope it represents them all and that no one will be offended by being excluded. It is our hope that a second volume on this subject will appear in the future. We certainly have the material for it!

Eldad Community Church

7

ACKNOWLEDGMENTS

At the risk of forgetting someone, we want to recognize the following people whose efforts made this book possible: Jammie Alber, who organized all the submissions into something resembling a book; Jarrett Medlin and Eric Syverson, who made the first selects; Jason Jenkins, Karen Stockman and Jim McCarty, who did the edits and filled in the holes; and especially all the people who took the time to send us the photos of their churches!

Conception Abbey, Conception

INTRODUCTION

A simple relaxing Sunday afternoon drive through any part of Missouri will show how important religion was to the state's founders. From the rugged Ozark hills and across the plains, churches dot the countryside. Missouri, being the center state of the United States, proudly displays the diversity of all parts of our country. In Missouri's cities there are grand cathedrals, synagogues, and mosques, as well as churches from every major denomination and nondenominational churches.

Among the collection of churches that we have in Missouri are those that not only represent a group of people who share a common belief, but those that also share a strong cultural bond. These include churches that were historically black and others that represent individual cultures, such as German, French, Italian, and even Swedish. Here the language of the old country is often still spoken.

Last but not least, as we mention religions around Missouri, we must not forget the large Amish and Mennonite communities that are tucked into the rural areas of the state. These communities are reminiscent of a forgotten way of life. Most have their own grocery stores, hardware stores, quilt shops, blacksmiths, and buggy repair. These communities have everything centrally located as some only travel by horse and buggy.

These religions and ways of life have the same root in the sixteenth century when they broke from the Catholic Church and became Anabaptist, claiming that infant baptism was not a way of salvation. Later, in 1693, the Amish split from the Mennonites and became known as the Old Order. The Mennonites were named after the founder of the Anabaptist faith, a former Catholic priest, Menno Simmons.

The Mennonites came to Missouri around the 1870s. The Amish came to Missouri as early as 1850, but none of the settlements that were established before 1930 are still in existence. Today, Amish communities are located near the following areas: Bowling Green, Clark, Jamesport, Seymour, and Versailles. Jamestown is the home of the largest Old Order Amish settlement west of the Mississippi.

St. Paul Lutheran Church, Slater

Sycamore Grove Mennonite Church, Garden City

Located near Garden City, Sycamore Grove Menno-nite Church was founded in 1882 by Amish and Mennonite families that had settled in rural Cass County in the 1850s. The church was built close to Clearfork Creek with timber on three sides, hence the name Sycamore Grove. The church building has gone through several renovations over the years, remodeling and adding on in 1924, 1950, and 1983.

Today Sycamore Grove is still a peaceful, scenic loca-tion surrounded by trees. The membership numbers around 160, with a normal Sunday's attendance of about 120; descendants of the original settlers still attend.

As we explore the churches around Missouri we will notice not only the architecture of buildings varying from small, simply built, rural churches to monumental struc-tures built from carved stone. We will also explore the people who are truly the church. We will take notice of the events that go along with church life in Missouri.

Were we to only focus on buildings, we would leave out all of the glorious places in Missouri where a person might find that he or she best communes with God.

Missouri started as the northern part of the Louisiana Territory with its strong French heritage. It is not surpris-ing, then, that the towns of Ste. Genevieve and St. Louis (as their names suggest) were large French Catholic com-munities and the homes of the first Catholic churches in the state. The first Catholic church was built in 1755 in the small town of Ste. Genevieve. Before this, a mission chapel was located in present-day St. Louis. It was led by a Cana-dian priest, who had come into the state with the intention of converting the American Indians to Catholicism as early as 1700.

Between that time and 1755, when the church was com-pleted in Ste. Genevieve, circuit priests ministered to the small Catholic congregations around the state several times a year. Until their arrival, congregations were dependent on their own means, studying and teaching the faith to one another.

Ste. Genevieve Catholic Church, Ste. Genevieve

The beautiful Ste. Genevieve Catholic Church is located in the old part of town. The cornerstone was laid April 20, 1876, and the fourteen-foot cross was placed atop the steeple on November 1, 1879. It stands on the site of the original log church believed to have been originally built near the river at Le Grand Champ around 1754 and moved to this site in 1794. A stone church later replaced it in 1837. The current church was built around that stone structure.

In an 1874 editorial in the Ste. Genevieve Fair Play calling for a new church to be built, the writer wrote: "Let us add to it a steeple that will tower and rise toward heaven, and a cross upon its summit that will overlook everything also made by the hands of men of our town, and shine with approbation to the surrounding country."

It was dedicated in 1880 and enlarged in 1911. The bell tower and steeple are an amazing 190 feet tall. The bell tower contains four bells. Painted statues in the church honor Mary, Christ, St. Paul, the apostles, and other saints. Stained-glass windows also depict biblical scenes and early leaders of the Church.

The second organized religion to come into Missouri was Protestant in nature, Baptist specifically. The first known Baptist sermon heard west of the Mississippi was in 1794 when a visiting pastor from Kentucky, Reverend Josiah Dodge, preached on Saline Creek near Ste. Genevieve. Another Protestant pastor, Reverend John Clark, who was Methodist and later converted to Baptist, was the first known pastor to go to what was then Spanish territory to convert the American settlers. When his appointments were met, he was threatened and asked to leave.

Possibly because of this threat, the desire for conversion increased, and in 1797, another Baptist preacher, Reverend Thomas Johnson, visited the Cape Girardeau area performing what would be the first Protestant baptism west of the Mississippi for Mrs. Agnes Ballew in Randall Creek. Not until 1803 was there actually a Protestant pastor who lived in the state. As a minister of the German Reformed Church of North Carolina, Reverend Samuel Weyberg organized meeting places and congregations in the Cape Girardeau district, even though there was not an actual church building built until later.

First Baptist Church, Glasgow

The following history is lettered on a sign on the grounds of Glasgow First Baptist Church: "The Baptist Church has had three sites. Old Chariton was organized 1820, with twenty members. 1827 was moved to Monticello; then 1861 to Glasgow where a substantial brick house was built and sold in 1866 to the Presbyterians. After some years the congregation erected the present building, one of the most elegant churches in the county, at a cost of $12,000. Dedicated in 1871."

Protestants continued their migration into Missouri from the southern states. They were not welcomed, but continued to fight to share their beliefs with the other inhabitants of the new state. Eventually permanent settlers came to make Missouri their homes, and these families welcomed the Protestants.

After the War of 1812, many Protestant missionaries came to the frontier. The faith grew in the rural areas as meetings were held in homes. Traveling missionaries were put on salaries by the small groups and started holding courts within the "church" to manage the conduct of the members. At this time blue laws were also established. Those who continued to work on the Sabbath were prosecuted as were individuals caught playing cards, billiards, swearing, and practicing idleness. Proof of punishment for these crimes is still found on the record books of many of the older counties.

Finally church buildings began to dot the landscape as Missouri took shape as a state. Permanence of the different congregations that had been meeting in homes was established as churches organized and buildings were constructed. Among those first churches were: Bethel Church in 1805 in the Tywappity Bottom, Fee Fee Baptist Church in 1807 near Pattonville in St. Louis County, Mount Zion Baptist Church in Boon's Lick in 1812, and by 1818, five churches had been organized, forming the Mount Pleasant Organization.

Methodist churches were also organizing at this time, the first at McKendree, close to Bethel Church. While there is little known about many of the early structures in Missouri, it is noted that this chapel was constructed of hewn poplar logs and is still standing. This congregation met at a chapel that was referred to as, "Old Camp Grounds" because it had been the home of many early-day camp meetings in the Cape Girardeau circuit. Reverend John Travis, a Methodist circuit pastor from Tennessee, was sent to Missouri in 1806 and was surprised to see Cape Girardeau and Meramec circuits already organized.

The Presbyterian organization took place as Reverend Salmon Giddings came to Missouri and traveled among the settled areas near the Mississippi gathering the remnant of earlier groups of Presbyterians. In August of 1816, he formed the first church in Belleview Valley near Potosi where four elders from a North Carolina church had settled in 1807.

Organization of the Protestant Episcopal faith and the Christian Church (Disciples of Christ) closely followed; the Protestant Episcopal faith in 1819, in St. Louis by the Reverend John Ward, and the Christian Church in 1817 by Elders Thomas McBride and Joel H. Haden. The Salt Creek Christian Church of Missouri was established in that year in Howard County. The Christian Church grew rapidly as pastors from Ohio and Kentucky moved into Missouri in the decade following the start of Salt Creek Christian Church.

The Mormons made their way into Missouri in 1831 led by Joseph Smith and settled in the area surrounding Independence. In the *Book of Mormon* this time is referred to as the, "land beautiful." The Mormons made up communities and lived on a social basis as opposed to an individual basis. They became economically successful and because of their numbers were able to elect those representing the Mormon way of thinking. This angered their neighbors and in 1833 the Mormons were pushed into Clay and Daviess counties, only to be followed by another ousting, in 1839, when they were driven into Illinois. Sites holy to the Morman faith continue to draw pilgrims to Missouri.

As Missouri was evolving and religions were being woven into the tapestry that would define her, German religious leaders began to migrate and started the Reformed Evangelical Church of Germany with two churches, one at Friedens and the other at Femme Osage in St. Charles County built by Herman Garlichs in 1834 and 1835.

Germans of the Orthodox Lutherans came in high numbers as 600 left their home country searching for religious freedom in 1839. Martin Stephan, a bishop, led them and became the pastor of St. John's Church in Dresden. This group established the towns of Altenburg and Wittenburg and also formed Concordia Seminary at Altenburg in 1839.

Trinity Lutheran Church, Freidheim

The town of Friedheim, originally Dissen, saw its first German Lutheran immigrants between 1830 and 1832. Few Lutherans lived in the area during these early years, so two or three neighboring Lutheran families gathered in each other's homes to hold worship services every Sunday.

As more Lutheran immigrants settled in the area, church services were held regularly in Bernard Guessenberg's home, which was the largest available.

In 1847, some twenty Lutheran families from Friedheim called their first pastor, Friedrich Julius Blitz. He was one of the first students to graduate from the seminary at Altenburg. Trinity Lutheran was organized the next year, and a log parsonage, which also served as a church and school, was built upon the present church property. In 1849, a log church with a schoolroom was built beside the parsonage. At this time, the bylaws for the new church were written and membership began to increase, mostly through immigrants from Germany.

In 1856, the congregation decided to build a larger church. The building was made of rough-hewn sandstone, which was hauled a quarter-mile to the building site by a yoke of oxen. Four oxen were required to move some of the larger stones. Today, the sandstone's origin still can be seen southwest of the church on County Road 419.

At the building site, the stones were put into place using planks laid against the walls. Long poles were used to lift the rocks into place. The cornerstone for the present stone church building was laid on May 6, 1857. The exterior of the church, with the exception of the steeple, entrance steps, windows, and roof replacements, stands firmly today after 148 years showing hardly any wear.

The church was remodeled in 1948. Its twenty-first pastor, the Reverend Roger Steinbrueck, is servicing Trinity Lutheran Church currently.

The Catholic faith, the first organized in Missouri, continued its growth and created the first state diocese at St. Louis in 1826. A second diocese with Kansas City as a cathedral city was established in 1880. Priests of the Roman Catholic churches were sent to minister to the Germans who had settled in large numbers. Parochial schools were built to educate the Catholic youth.

As times changed so did the churches. Slavery issues in the nation affected Missouri where slaves and slave owners had always attended the same churches. The slave community began to pull away from these churches and establish their own in the 1850s. Following the Civil War, when slaves gained their freedom, black churches organized.

13

Washington Avenue Baptist Church, Springfield

This is the second home to Springfield's oldest African-American congregation. It was listed on the National Register of Historic Places in December of 2000. This church sits on Drury Campus and was moved brick by brick across the street to make room for another campus building.

The first Jewish church was established in Missouri in 1836. This congregation was made up mostly of German and Polish immigrants. The Jews had not been allowed to live in the area when it was Spanish territory, but were able to move into Missouri after the Louisiana Purchase. The first organized church was in St. Louis, followed by the Sons of the Covenant. A group of B'nai El withdrew and organized Temple Israel in 1886. After the Civil War Jewish congregations were formed in St. Joseph, Sedalia, Kansas City, and other areas around the state.

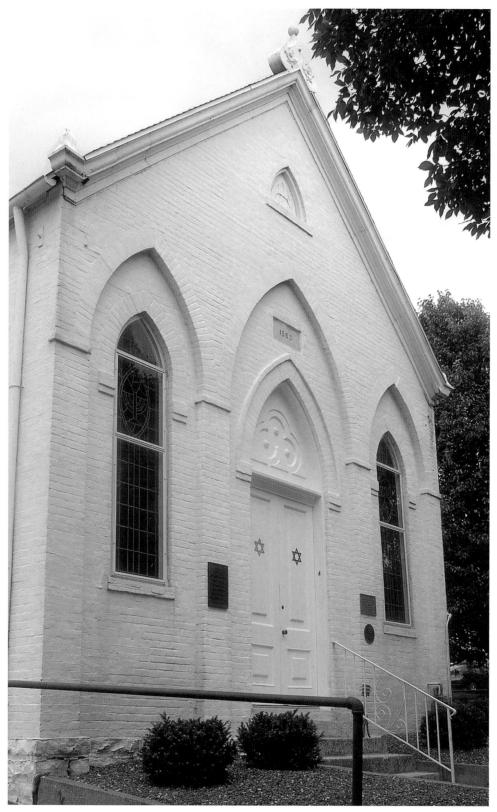

Tempel Beth El, Jefferson City

Built in 1883 and said to be the oldest Jewish temple in continuous use west of the Mississippi, Jefferson City's Tempel Beth El is home to a small but devoted Jewish congregation. Members drive from all parts of central Missouri to attend one of the few temples located outside Missouri's metropolitan areas. Lay people lead the Friday services, with rabbis from Columbia performing weddings or funerals.

In the 1926 census, the value of church buildings was estimated at a little over ten times that of the average rural building. Religion was firmly established in Missouri.

Chapter 1

An Old Testament

I come to this place
To pray, worship and be fed
To center my life
And continue spirit-led

To commune with others
And fellowship so sweet
As collectively we join
In devotion at Jesus' feet
—LCK 2006

As the state began to take form, religion became the backbone of each community. This section displays the churches that in many cases have been standing in our cities, towns, and rural areas for more than one hundred years. In several instances, as you will see, the church came first and the town was built around it as groups of people with a shared faith settled the different regions of the state.

St. Joachim Catholic Church, Old Mines

Founded in 1723, the Old Mines church began as a mission church to Ste. Genevieve. The present church building at Old Mines was built in 1830, making it the oldest Catholic Church still standing west of the Mississippi. When the church was consecrated by Bishop Joseph Rosati sermons were preached in both English and in French. In 1820, Pere Pratte of Ste. Genevieve had built a log church here. Up until that time visiting priests from Fort de Chartres, Prairie du Rocher, Ste. Genevieve and Perryville Seminary, had said the Mass in miner's homes and outside at the various camps spread out in the country between Le Richwoods, La Mine a' Valle, La Vieille Mine and Mine au Breton.

In 1828, Father Jean Bouillier started the brick church, commissioning Obadiah Freeman to supervise making the bricks from clay at Adrian Coleman's land grant. Bouillier left to travel to the motherhouse in Paris, France, in 1830, and the church was finished by Father Philip Borgna, C.M., and consecrated by Bishop Joseph Rosati on October 9, 1831, with sermons preached in English and French. The original floor plan was 30 feet by 110 feet, with a 50-foot high steeple.

The first Diocesan priest, John Cotter, took over in 1841. Father Cotter, killed in a fall from a horse in 1851, is buried in a brick tomb under the floor of the church to the left of the stairs; a bronze marker was added on his tomb location in 1995.

Father James Fox took over the parish after Cotter was killed, and served until 1868. He oversaw an enlargement and modification of the floor plan of the church in 1852 to 1857, adding the wings and enlarging the rectangular steeple. These modifications were capped off with the purchase of the cast 960-pound steeple bell for $351.30 by Mary Lewis Lamarque in 1858. A visit to the attic shows the original 1850s wood shingles nailed to hewn and pegged roof truss members. The nineteenth-century church had pairs of chimneys on either side, for stoves used to heat the building.

The church was renovated at least three times in the twentieth century: once in about 1900, once in 1945, and the last time in the 1960s. During the 1945 restorations, the chimneys were removed, but the original stone altar was restored.

First United Methodist Church of New Madrid

Presiding Elder Jesse Walker founded the First United Methodist Church in 1810. John Scripps is noted as the first pastor for the 30 members. Following the New Madrid Earthquake of 1811–12, attendance grew to more than 150 members. Since its beginning the church has been served by 70 pastors. Records show the following amounts paid to the preachers in charge of the circuit during the years mentioned: 1821—$37.25; 1825—$16.45; 1826—$19.37; and 1830—$79.

New Madrid, located in the Bootheel of Missouri and the First United Methodist Church, 627 Mill Street, have withstood earthquakes, floods, war, and fire and have not yet been defeated. The spirit and faith of its Christian pioneer ancestors continue to guide and lead the church in its mission in the community.

Pleasant Green Methodist Church, Pleasant Green

Organized in 1825 in Pleasant Green by M. B. Evans and a group of people in the Walker neighborhood; charter members were Winston Walker, Polly Walker, Samuel Walker, Nancy Walker, Peter B. and Sallie Cockrell, Laban and Lucy Johnson, Samuel and Margaret Forbes, and Ruben Walker. This group had services in their homes until they built a log meetinghouse, which was the first Methodist church west of St. Louis County. The second building was raised in 1863. The present building was built in 1868 and dedicated by Dr. David R. McAnally, co-founder of Central Methodist College.

From 1954 to 1960, the interior underwent remodeling and redecorating. A church kitchen and dining area were built near the church; double doors were added along with a concrete porch and steps.

Old Auxvasse Presbyterian Church, Auxvasse

The first building of this congregation was a hewn-log structure. Today's building is a white-clapboard church that was built in 1870. Members of the famous Boone family started this church and it is the second oldest Presbyterian congregation west of the Mississippi. It is also the site where elders sat to discuss establishing Fulton's Westminster College.

One of the early couples of the church was Sherwood and America Maddox who traveled in a cart pulled by a team of oxen and a blind horse. As most members came in wagons, it was said that horse-trading often took place after services and that a person might not leave with the same animals.

The building has had many changes over the years. It is no longer heated with a wood stove that had to be stoked up a few hours before the service to ensure warmth. Another change was the removal of the wall that went down the middle of the sanctuary, dividing men from women during worship.

Mt. Horeb Baptist Church, Mineola

The home of Samuel Boone, nephew of Daniel Boone, was the first home of this church when it was organized in August of 1833. The first members were Samuel Boone, Willis Hawkins, Jesse Vancleave, John Gregory, Benjamin Bousher, Ann Boone, Mary Hawkins, Lucy Vancleave, Elisabeth Gregory, Mary Bousher, Sarah Ann Carter, and "Susan, a woman of colour." Other family names connected to the history are Cole, Tate, Davis, Sheets, Kettle, Hays, Hampton, Morrow, Stewart, Ford, Naughton, Thompson, Snethen, Payne, Atterberry, and Lewellen. Reverend Elder Coates was the first pastor.

Early church meetings lasted for weeks at a time and congregation members camped on the ground. They would hunt wildlife for meals. One of these meetings was held in the winter and a great revival was experienced. Even though the temperatures were sub-zero the congregation gathered on the banks of Prairie Fork where they built a large log heap, set it afire and cut the ice. The pastor led candidates into the water to baptize them as brethren and sisters stood on the banks and sang, "Brethren, if your hearts are warm, ice and snow will do no harm."

Mt. Horeb was originally organized as a Baptist Church but is now non-denominational. It was placed on the National Register of Historic Places in1980. The church still has an old stile block in the front, which was used for ladies who rode sidesaddle. The original church building was a double log structure with a lean-to at both ends. The present building is one large high ceiling room with a wood stove, rough sawed plank for flooring. The pews are hand-hewed sycamore. There are three windows on each side with a diamond-shaped pane at top of each. At the back and along one side are the names of all pastors and deacons. The history and photos of events of the church are posted. In the pulpit area is a lectern and a piano. A double door faces to the south and a single door to the east side of the pulpit area.

Femme Osage United Church of Christ, Femme Osage

Femme Osage United Church of Christ has the distinction of being the first Pentecostal parish west of the Mississippi; it was founded in 1833. The village of Femme Osage is one of the last small hamlets left in the ever-developing St. Charles County. The parish property also consists of a stone one-room schoolhouse and two cemeteries. The town is located in a valley along a small creek. There is a general store, now closed, and several homes. The present church was built in 1888.

Assumption Catholic Church, Cedron

The oldest of its denomination in Moniteau County, this church was one of the seven founded by Father Ferdinand Helias. Of the seven, it is the only one that is not an active parish, having fallen victim to the loss of population during the farm crisis of the 1980s. The first building was a log structure that measured thirty by thirty-two feet. It was first known as Cedron Church, then Becker's Church and later Assumption Catholic Church, Cedron.

In 1867–1872 a new building was built, a thirty-by-fifty-foot brick church. In 1903 a thirty-one-foot addition was added, including a bell tower and a sanctuary. In 1914, new windows and metal ceiling were added and are in the process of being restored. The last regular mass was held in August of 1993. The building is still used for weddings, funerals, and Christmas masses.

Old Presbyterian Church, Potosi

This red brick building on Breton Street in Potosi is the oldest Presbyterian church west of the Mississippi River having been built in 1832. It now houses a museum. The cemetery behind the church houses many beautiful gravestones including that of Moses Austin, who founded Potosi and is also considered the "grandfather of Texas" for his role in settling that state. The cracks on the tomb were made by Texans in 1938 when they wanted to move the body of Moses Austin to Texas. They sent an undertaker and a hearse to Potosi. The undertaker was discovered chipping away at the tomb. The town marshal was called and the Texan sent packing. A few weeks later the Texas governor sent his secretary of state to Potosi with a public apology for the incident.

High Point Baptist Church, Leeton

This is the oldest church in Johnson County and was started two years before the organization of the county. It was organized in June of 1832 with twenty-eight members and Elder John T. Rickets as pastor. Services at that time were held on Saturday and Sunday once a month.

The current building was erected in 1881 on five acres that were purchased for $30 an acre. When this information was submitted in August of 2006, one of the current deacons, Norman Powers, had been in attendance for more than eighty-one years of his life and indirectly for the nine months he was carried, as his mother was a member. Services are still held in this church in Leeton.

First United Methodist Church, Jefferson City

Four men came together in Jefferson City in 1837 from places near and far to organize this church: Peter McCain from Ireland, John Curry from Virginia, and Jesse Waldron and William Kerr from Tennessee. The first pastor was Jesse Bennet. Two years later the church built the first building, but soon after the Methodist Church divided into two denominations, the north and the south. First United Methodist was a member of the Methodist Episcopal Church, South.

During the Civil War the church was under the control of the Union and almost died out completely. After the war the church began to thrive and built a new building next to the original in 1874. By the 1890s, the church had grown to the point that yet another larger facility was needed. In 1898 Arthur Barnes was appointed pastor and the new building was built under his leadership. Later additions include the Carson Annex in the 1950s and the Christian Life Center in 1984.

23

Immanuels United Church of Christ, Holstein

This predominantly German congregation met in a small log church, originally named German Lutheran Church on Charette. In 1847 Reverend Joseph Rieger was called as the first full-time pastor. The log church burned in 1885 and a new brick structure was built. In 1884 a larger brick building was built with a basement to accommodate the school. A Sunday school addition was built in the 1960s and a kitchen in the 1990s.

The name was changed in 1884 to German Evangelical Immanuels Church at Holstein. After a merger of the Evangelical and Reformed denominations the name was Immanuels E and R Church and in 1957, the E and R and Congregational denominations merged and became the United Church of Christ.

St. Paul's Evangelical Lutheran Church, Concordia

Freedom Township in Lafayette County was the home of early German Lutherans and later became present day Concordia. Heinrich Christian Liever became the leader of the church that organized shortly after he was asked to baptize the children of the Lutherans. At first the congregation conducted services in the member's homes where they would sing hymns and read a sermon from a book. These were called reading services.

The first building was built in 1844 when John Henry Bruns donated an acre of land. The building was built of logs and was twenty by eighteen feet. On July 18, 1842, the 10 members agreed to dedicate the house of worship as St. Paul's Evangelical Lutheran Church. The original acre where the first building stood is part of the church cemetery.

In 1860 the church built its first brick building and enlarged that building in 1880. The congregation increased over the years and by 1884 numbered 1,236. It was easy to see that a larger building was needed. J. M. E. Riedell of Fort Wayne, Indiana, was hired as architect and H. Bererfoerden of Kansas City, Missouri as the contractor.

The shape of the church building makes a Greek cross and is in Gothic style. The church celebrated in 2005 the one-hundred-year anniversary of the sanctuary. Today the church is still used for regular worship services, weddings, funerals, and other events. The membership as of January 1, 2006 was 1,713. The church supports the K–8 St. Paul's Lutheran School. His Little Lambs Child Development Center provides daycare for preschoolers and after-school care. Concordia is also home to St. Paul's High School.

Paradise United Methodist Church, Paradise

The original meeting place was in the Corum School near Smithville led by Reverend E. M. Marion and Amos Tutt. In December 1868 a building was built in Gosneyville where the church had moved. Trustees at the time were Ben Taul, W. M. Murray, Charles McGhee, T. J. Ellington, William Sparks, John Rollins, and G. W. Douglas.

A parsonage was built for the Gosneyville Methodist Evangelical Church in 1881 when an adjoining lot was purchased. Gosneyville became Paradise in 1884 and the church followed suit by changing its name. In the late 1800s the church burned and a new building went up in 1903. Since that time an aging steeple was replaced in the early 1970s and in 1999 a family center and running water were added. Recent construction increased the space with new classrooms and an expansion of the family center.

Wilderness Church, Silver Dollar City, Branson

Settlers near Reeds Spring built the one-room log church in 1847. It was originally used as a county church and school and later became the Evangelistic Center and community building for Reeds Spring and Galena. In 1960 the church was dismantled, log by log, and moved to Silver Dollar City Amusement Park where it was reconstructed.

The site where it now sits, a hillside overlooking the White River Valley, was chosen by the park employees, but was first rejected by park founder Mary Herschend because a massive white oak would have to be cut down. The staff came up with a solution that the tree could serve as the pulpit. Lester Vining, one of Silver Dollar City's most famous early citizens, carved the huge trunk into a six-hundred-pound pulpit.

Today visitors to the park can go in and participate in singing of hymns and church services. It is also a favorite place for weddings. The church is open during park hours unless there is a ceremony in process.

First Baptist Church, Springfield

The mission of this historic Springfield church is to "Worship God, Reach the Lost, Build Strong Families, and Encourage and Equip Believers for Service." It is located at 815 East St. Louis Street.

St. Lawrence Church, New Hamburg

The first church of St. Lawrence in New Hamburg was a log church finished late in 1848. Parishioners wanted to save a piece of their heritage. In 1978, Father Francis Donovan, pastor of St. Lawrence, started the renovation of the old church. Siding (asphalt and wood) was removed from the exterior walls. Shown here is a picture of the old church after the removal of the siding. Repairs made to the first church included replacing and repairing logs, replacing and repairing chinking, putting a preservative on logs, reworking windows, replacing a door frame, and making a new gable. The roof was removed, existing decking repaired (or replaced), felt underlayment put down and fire-retardant treated cedar shakes and flashing added. On the interior of the building the logs were repaired and a preservative treatment added. The exterior of the church was covered with boards to protect the logs. Parishioners donated most of the labor restoring the old church.

Mt. Zion Christian Church, Palmyra

On the last day of April, 1858, a deed was recorded in Palmyra of one acre and sixteen poles from Armistead and Juliet Kemper to the trustees of the Mt. Zion Church: Thomas Paschal, John R. Withers, and Wesley L. Taylor. There were about fifty charter members. The building was a long brick structure and was erected by Elisha Grant.

The brick was made close by and forest trees were hewn for supports. When a new building was later needed, the same timbers were used and still remain. As was customary at the time, the church was made with two front doors, one for men and the other for women and children. Originally there was also a section in the back of the church for slaves. A basement was used for Sunday school classes and during the week subscription schools were held.

Dignitaries of the membership included Moses Bates, one of Hannibal's founders and also U.S. Representative William Henry Hatch. Church membership required adherence to strict rules. Congregation members were removed for reasons including drunkenness and disorderly walking. Membership could be restored after a public acknowledgement of the offense. A Civil War skirmish was fought near the church on December 28, 1861.

C. A. Bartholomew, an architect from St. Louis, was called to design and erect a new building in 1892 at the cost of $3,000. Reverend J. H. Harrison from St. Louis dedicated the building on November 20, 1892; the pastor at the time was William M. Roe.

Although the present-day church is a Gothic style and includes a bell tower, it has never held a bell. The sanctuary is bathed with sun from three sunburst-patterned stained-glass windows. Carved wooden pews and the vaulted wooden ceiling of the present building were moved from the original 1859 structure.

Hope United Church of Christ, Cosby

Swiss immigrants, numbering about forty, whose descendents still make up a large part of the congregation, came together in 1854 to organize this church. All in the same year, they had traveled across the Atlantic, landed in New Orleans, sailed up the Mississippi and Missouri Rivers to St. Joseph to join other Swiss immigrants who arrived in 1840.

First worship services were held a few miles south of Savannah in various homes though now Hope United Church of Christ is in Cosby. Even though the congregation was ministered to by several evangelists of different creeds, they kept to and instructed their children in their Reformed doctrine.

Hope Church was incorporated with the Reformed Church in 1865 and became Hope Evangelical and Reformed Church. A frame building was built in 1869 on the current site and replaced in 1914. An educational wing was added in 1954. In 1957 the name became Hope United Church of Christ after the merger between the Evangelical and Reformed and the Congregational Christian Churches created the United Church of Christ.

First Christian Church (Disciples of Christ), Warrensburg

In 1855 Warrensburg was incorporated and a Christian Church was organized in the Courthouse. In 1859 the congregation built a large brick building on West Gay Street. During the Civil War, the members scattered and the trustee was forced to sell the building to pay the debt that was owed. When the war ended members came back and met for a while at the home of A. H. Gilkeson who later purchased a lot on the south side of West Gay Street and donated it for a new building. With funds that remained from the sale of the first building, a new white frame building was erected.

David Nation was hired as pastor and several years later married a young widow, Carry Amelia Moore Gloyd, who gained lasting notoriety as Carry A. Nation, the hatchet-welding prohibitionist. The first full-time pastor was George W. Longan with a succession of many pastors who stayed for short periods. Included in these was John Anderson Brooks, a temperance orator who preached on Sundays and waged a temperance campaign during the week. He ran for governor of Missouri in 1888 and was a candidate for vice-president on a Prohibition ticket.

In the mid-1880s the congregation had grown and a new building was needed. The congregation still worships in the 117-year-old church that has been vigilantly maintained.

Peaksville Christian Church, Revere

On February 18, 1956, several men and their families met at the home of James Christy to discuss starting a Christian Church. Later that year it was decided to build a church at the corners of Lafayette and East. Mrs. Peake, founder of the town, deeded over lots 5, 6, 7, and 8 for the church. It was completed and dedicated in September of 1857.

The church building has been destroyed twice, by a tornado in 1870 and by lightning strike and fire in 1922, but the congregation grew and persevered in their faith. The original building was brick and had hand hewn pews without backs. The second building was wood and had the customary two entrances, one for women and small children and the other for older boys and men. A three-foot partition separated the church inside. Hannah Christy, wife of the first board chairman, James Christy, donated the bell for the church.

The following has been passed down from the early church on a torn piece of paper from around the time that the decision was made to build a church; it was with minutes from what appears to have been a business meeting that listed names and amounts pledged to fund the new church. It is unclear exactly what the purpose of this sheet was. Perhaps it was a checklist to make sure that all were in agreement with doctrine.

What shall we do to be Saved

Believe	D. Starr
Du as the Bible saiz	Price
Repent and be Baptized	Salyers
Repent and be Baptized	J. Shaffer
Arise and be Baptized	J. E. Davidson
Serve the Truth and be Baptized	Ervilians
Serve the Truth and be Baptized	Henson Mossey

Swearing Jury
Martin Kious, witness
Wm. Price
Owen Hamit
J. E. Davidson

Zion Church, Arrow Rock

This church in Arrow Rock was built by the Cumberland Presbyterian Church; in 1900 the building was bought by the Evangelical Congregation which held English and German services until 1930 when the congregation became Zion United Church of Christ. Because of a declining membership, the last service was held on Christmas Eve 2005.

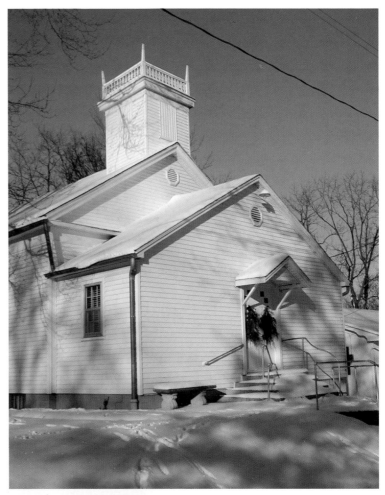

Calumet Church, Calumet

Originally a community church and organized as a Presbyterian church in 1857, Calumet was named for the town. The following are a list of individuals who signed the constitution set forth when the church organized: John Turner, James W. Griffith, Ellen Griffith, Martha Turner, Melinda Butts, Susan H. Boyd, Rachel Estes, Cyrus Mackey, Charlotte Mackey, Matthew Treadway, Melinda Venable, Sarah Wilcoxen, and Ivan Venable. Many of the charter members have descendents who are still active in the church.

The original building was a log structure, but in 1871 it was deemed to be in bad condition and unsafe. The church, not having the funds to build or repair, requested to be dissolved.

The petition was granted and members were attached to Buffalo and Corinth congregations. The church reorganized in 1888 and erected the current building with the exception of the Sunday school room in back, which was added at a later date.

Our Lady Help of Christians, Frankenstein

The friendly town of Frankenstein is the home of this parish that was organized in 1863 and has been in three different locations: on a wooded knoll, in a valley, and on a high ridge. The original name was Mary, Help of Christians. The current building was a combination of church, school and convent. It was started in September of 1922 and was completed in 1923. The exterior and the bell tower are of quarried limestone and the roof is red Italian tile. The stone was quarried about a mile from the church and was brought in by teams and wagons. The stones were lifted in place by a mule. Most of the construction labor was donated by parishioners. The main altar in the church is Carthage marble. The church has a membership of about ninety families.

First Baptist Church, Vandalia

This church in Vandalia was originally organized under the name New Michigan Baptist Church and met in the New Michigan School that was located just south of the present town. The church met in this schoolhouse until 1872 when it moved into the community and met in the public school house and then in the Presbyterian Church building. In 1874 the first building was built. It was a one-room brick structure. The name was then changed to the Vandalia Baptist Church until 1954 when it was incorporated as First Baptist Church.

The current sanctuary was built in 1900–1901 and was dedicated September 29–October 2, 1901. An educational building was added in 1954. The first Baptist Church is a charter member of the Audrain Baptist Association. It is also a part of the Missouri Baptist Association and the Southern Baptist Convention.

M. E. Church. Schell City, Mo. 4758

United Methodist Church, Schell City

The Methodist Episcopal Church started on January 2, 1872. The name was later changed. The group met in a railroad depot then moved to the Robinson Schoolhouse. In 1878 a building was built that still stands today. A church annex was built in 1921.

Knox Presbyterian Church, Gentry

This church is three miles north of Gentry and was built by nine families who migrated to the area from Ayr, Canada. It has been in continuous use for more than 125 years.

First Baptist Church, Desloge

In 1877 a wood-chopping Baptist preacher named Wann came to the farm of Mr. Sam Orten and the farm of Mr. and Mrs. Ben Goode to chop cordwood. He asked permission from the Ortenville School District to hold religious services in the schoolhouse. The services resulted in a revival and following the revival a group met and organized the Ortenville Baptist Church.

Charter members of the church were brothers Riley Gibson and George Gibson, Misses Elizabeth and Ida Gibson, Mr. and Mrs. Ellis B. Cunningham, Mr. and Mrs. Robert Lawson, Frank McClanahan, Henry Price, Henry White, Mr. and Mrs. James Reeder, and Mr. Yakley. Riley Gibson, Frank McClanahan, and

Ellis B. Cunningham were elected to serve as the first deacons with George Gibson as first clerk. Regular services and a brush arbor revival were held during the summers. The schoolhouse burned in 1893 and in 1894 a new building was started at the corner of Lincoln and Locust Streets. When the church moved to the new building the name was changed to Desloge Baptist Church.

With a new pastor, Dr. J. H. Winstead, came changes to the building in 1931. The north section of the building had the ceiling lowered, which made room for two more classrooms. During the Depression years the pastor and men of the church worked with their hands and excavated through almost solid rock to make a full basement and install a new central heating system.

The sanctuary was remodeled in 1938 under the leadership of J. R. Wagoner, a baptistery was added and Mrs. W. A. Buckner painted a mural over the baptistery. In 1968 a completely new building was begun. The church was completed in 1969 and the dedication ceremony was held on August 10, 1969.

The First Baptist Church is a member of the Mineral Area Baptist Association, and the Missouri State Convention. The highest Sunday school membership was 652 in 1934.

St. Paul's Episcopal Church, Lee's Summit

Three women saw the need for a church in Lee's Summit. These ladies, Elizabeth Whiting, Belle Torres, and Bessie Batrell, raised the money needed by sewing and selling carpet rags. Although these three are credited with this endeavor all the way through choosing the plans, signing the contract, overseeing construction, and paying the bills, there were originally five women in the sewing circle. The land for the church was donated by William B. Howard, founder of Lee's Summit, on July 16, 1884. The town was in a state of growth at the time with the addition of the Missouri Pacific Railroad. Reverend Fredrick B. Scheetz, a former railroad surveyor, designed and donated the plans.

The church was built to twenty-four by forty feet with twelve-foot sides and twenty-eight feet to the apex of the roof. The walls and ceiling were paneled with the sides of railroad boxcars used in the Civil War. The cost of the church was $1,100 with a debt of only $200, which was paid off after five years. The first service was conducted by the Right Reverend Charles Robertson, bishop of the Diocese of Missouri, in November of 1884.

Saint Paul's was placed on the National Historic Register in 1985 and has been a stop on the Lee's Summit historic holiday house tour.

Immanuel Lutheran Church, Lincoln

Immanuel Lutheran Church is located in rural Benton County, northeast of Lincoln on "the prairie." The congregation was founded in 1898 and was a daughter congregation of Mt. Zion Lutheran in Lincoln. In 1912 the cornerstone of the present church was set in place. Immanuel is affiliated with the Missouri Synod.

Fortuna United Methodist Church, Fortuna

The first service of the Fortuna United Methodist Church was held in a lumberyard belonging to William Ferguson and was conducted by E. D. C. Koeth of the Tipton Methodist Church. Many conversions were made. P. J. Schmidt donated the ground, $50 in cash, and the materials at cost to any denomination that would build the first church in Fortuna.

The Fortuna United Methodist Church, originally the Methodist Episcopal Church, organized and started building on October 1, 1901. The building was finished in the summer of 1902 and dedication services were held on the second Sunday of July 1904 when the debt of the building had been paid. In the beginning the building was used by not only the Methodist congregation, but also the Baptist and Christian Churches. Sunday school was a combination of the three denominations, but all had their own time for worship services.

After two additions had been added to the church and the one-hundred-year anniversary had been celebrated the church was stuck by lightning and the sanctuary burned. As you can see in the picture, the flames when the photo was taken resembled a cross. This inspired the church in spite of the heartbreak of their loss and one year later their first service was held in a new sanctuary.

St. Matthew Lutheran Church, Concordia

This church is in Concordia, but is referred to as the Ernestville church. It is named for the small community that existed many years ago consisting of the church, parsonage, and store, which is now a residence. The church of mostly German heritage was added onto in 1926. The church still has an active congregation.

St. Mary's Catholic Church, Adair

A crude log church was erected in 1870. Later a frame building was built and then the current building, where the church was organized and dedicated by Cardinal Glennon, archbishop at the time. This church is located thirteen miles east of Kirksville. At the time of the dedication, the parish consisted of 428 souls. Daughter parishes include Baring, Kirksville, and Memphis.

The current building was built by John Batwarth of Edina in 1904–1905. The church stands on a limestone and brick foundation and the framework is constructed of pine. The original wooden shake roof has been restored. The bell tower is fifty feet in height, but at one time was ninety feet until a severe storm destroyed it. Inside the church is a statue, "The Sorrowful Mother," one of only three ever produced from the original in Rome, Italy.

In December of 1972, it was announced that masses would discontinue for the winter. The congregation at this time was five couples of retirement age, seven men and women who had lost their mates or never married and four children. The masses were never resumed. The church was placed on the National Register of Historic Places on December 16, 1974.

Church of God, Bennett Spring State Park

This church sits in the middle of Bennett Spring State Park near Lebanon. Owner of this property was William Sherman Bennett. He had a vision that God wanted a church to be built on the property of the small community that was occupied by only three families that lived around the spring valley: Brice, Bennett, and Bolds.

The Bolds had moved to the valley from Indiana in 1893. George Bolds was an evangelist and he conducted annual camp meetings in the valley. He would preach and his wife and three daughters would sing. One night George was sick and unable to preach so he had his oldest daughter, Louise, preach at the meeting. This started her preaching ministry and she became known as Aunt Louise or Mother Bennett after her marriage to William Sherman Bennett in 1894. In 1917 during one of the camp meetings the Lord gave Sherman the vision to build a church. The first service was held in late 1917 and the building was dedicated to God. Mother (Louise) Bennett was the pastor until 1924 when the state bought the property that would later become the park, with the exception of the one acre where the church stood.

Another vision would save the church that had become unoccupied for some time. B. J. Usery built the first fish hatchery and was an operator at the spring branch mill; his son Ralph married Willa Jean Evans in 1939 and it was she who had this third vision. During World War II rationing of gasoline, tires, etc., contributed to the ceasing of regular services and with this, the deterioration in the structure.

In 1945 Willa Jean had a vision to restore the church and begin a Sunday school class. In 1985 she was honored for the vision and her forty years of service. She was still teaching toddlers in her seventies. Her funeral marked the highest attendance in the history of the church.

Over the years the church has added a bell tower, an extension for the stage area, bathrooms, sandstone rock veneer on the outside, a parsonage, a fellowship hall, pastor's office, and Sunday school rooms. Visitors are always welcome and often include campers and anglers, some even sporting fishing waders!

Longview Chapel Christian Church Disciples of Christ, Lee's Summit

This church was originally named the Longview Chapel. Lumber baron R. A. Long built this chapel at the main gate of this sixteen-hundred-acre farm in Lee's Summit. The Long family was generous, kind, and spiritual and Mr. Long felt the importance of providing a church, school, and community building for the workers who lived on the farm. He worked with the school superintendent as they made a one-room school in the church. The children walked to class or were delivered by wagon. The school was open for about five years until a motorized bus was purchased to take the children to neighboring public schools.

Every week, a projector was set up in the basement and a movie was shown. Teas, lectures, and book reviews also took place in the chapel. Skits and plays brought in large crowds. The chapel has been in use by the congregation and community since 1915 and is still a favored place for weddings. Upon the death of founder and builder R. A. Long in 1934, the church and financial responsibilities became that of the congregation. At this time the chapel was renamed as Longview Chapel Christian Church, DOC. The chapel was added to the National Registry of Historic Places in the early 1980s.

St. Mary the Virgin, Aldermanbury, Fulton

Few houses of worship can claim the history of the Church of St. Mary the Virgin, Aldermanbury, an English Church designed by Sir Christopher Wren in 1667. Originally built in London and today located on the campus of Westminster College in Fulton, the church is a popular site for weddings.

The church was destroyed by German bombs during World War II. In 1969, the ruins of the church were gathered up, moved to Missouri and rebuilt as a memorial to Winston Churchill and his historic "Sinews of Peace" address. It is now the home of the Winston Churchill Memorial and Library.

In 1946, with President Truman and other dignitaries in attendance, Churchill spoke of an "iron curtain" descending across Europe in a speech delivered at the Westminster College campus. Churchill's life, his visit to Fulton, and his seminal address are celebrated in a museum located beneath the church.

In 1990, Churchill's granddaughter, artist Edwina Sandys, unveiled a sculpture created from a section of the Berlin Wall and located just beyond the church. Christened "Breakthrough," the artwork features vibrant graffiti on its West Berlin side, while the Communist East Berlin surface shows only gray concrete.

Chapter

2

A NEW TESTAMENT

Lord, I feel your presence all around
Your beauty in nature, from sky to ground
Your Comforter when times are tough
What I do for You can't be enough
You gave Your life to purchase mine
I am a branch, You are The Vine
Take my life, live through me
Once was blind, but now I see
—LCK 2006

While nearly all of Missouri's congregations can claim a historic beginning, most have moved to the future by building new churches when the old structures no longer met their needs or when fire, tornados, or floods destroyed the original church. Besides bringing creature comforts to their members, these new churches combined architecture, stained glass, and works of art to assist the pastors in delivering the message of worship.

Many of Missouri's modern-day churches would amaze their original founders, bringing new ways to worship that could not have been dreamed of in the early days of statehood. Today's worshippers might listen to a sermon via a satellite link, then fellowship after the service in a coffee shop located in the church basement.

Cornerstone World Outreach Center, Springfield

The Cornerstone World Outreach Center in Springfield is an old building with a modern feel. The church began holding services in 1979 and met in the Stone Chapel on the Drury University campus until 1985 when the congregation purchased thirteen acres at Elfindale. A wooded lane takes the approximately eight hundred worshippers back to the church, which is also a Sky Angel satellite ministry.

St. John's Lutheran Church, Westboro

St. John's Lutheran Church (ELCA) is a rural church located seven miles west of the city of Westboro in north-central Atchison County. The church was founded on July 3, 1886, by a group of German immigrants who came from several villages around Osnabruck, Germany. The founding families of St. John's began emigrating from Germany in the early 1870s and continued into the 1880s.

A list of the names of the founding fathers of St. John's are: Henry Beckmann, Gerry Broermann, William Broermann, Herman Fuelling, William Fuelling, Fritz Hanrath, Gerry Horstman, Henry Kahle, Karl Kemper, Fred Klute, Adam Laumann, Gerry Laumann, H. W. Laumann, Henry J. Niemann, Herman Redeker, C. R. Rolf, Henry Rolf, Henry Schroeder, Adam Tiemann, Henry Tiemann, John Henry Vette Sr., and Jacob Zwick.

When the founding families arrived in Atchison County they shared the heritage of the German language and the Lutheran Protestant religion. At first the people traveled ten to twenty miles to Rock Port to worship at the Lutheran church there. Then, in 1882, arrangements were made for the pastor to travel to the home of William Broermann, where services were held.

Then on July 16, 1885, St. John's congregation was officially organized. Building plans were made, monetary commitments were secured, and construction began on a new church. The building was soon completed and on July 4, 1886, the new church building was dedicated.

The congregation continued to grow, so on April 27, 1941, at a special congregational meeting, it was decided that a new, larger building was needed. The money was raised and ground was broken on November 3, 1941, for the new church building. The cornerstone was laid on April 12, 1942, and the present church building was dedicated on December 13, 1942.

During the 120-year history of St. John's only eleven pastors have served the congregation. The names of each pastor and the dates they served St. John's are: B. Sickel, 1886–1889; J. G. Groenmiller, 1889–1893; Otto Roehrig, 1893–1897; William Harder, 1897–1906; H. Wieken, 1906–1912; R. Schemmelpfenning, 1912–1916; Dr. F. C. Nolte, 1916–1958; Fred Pederson, 1959–1964; Paul H. G. Moessner, 1965–1966; John R. Chandler, 1967–1976; and Richard Pearson, 1978 to the present. Presently St. John's is the only rural church in Atchison County that is self-supporting and has a full time pastor.

Many of the people who are members of St. John's today are descendants of the founding families of the congregation. There are now sixth- and seventh-generation families that attend church here. However as time has passed the congregation has become more diverse. Being located in the extreme corner of the state, the membership comes from at least ten communities and the rural area surrounding them in Missouri, Iowa, and Nebraska. Unique for a rural congregation today, the congregation is growing. At present there are 361 members with an average Sunday attendance of about 150. As it was in the early years of the congregation, St. John's continues to be a focal point of the community.

First Baptist Church, Camdenton

Originally located in Linn Creek, this church moved to Camdenton when the Lake of the Ozarks was constructed and Linn Creek was flooded. The original bell was taken to the new building, and then later to yet another building. First Baptist is in the process of building a new building now to meet the needs of the area's growing population.

Sacred Heart Catholic Church, Salem

This church in Salem has a stunning campus and recently had some updates, including tile and carpeting to make the sanctuary more acoustic. The St. Dorothy's Guild also is a new addition to the church. This group has made a mission of making the entire city block into a beautiful display of God's creation.

Faith United Church, St. Joseph

The story of this church is one of three different faiths coming together under one roof. In 1961 First Reformed, Trinity Evangelical, and First Congregational Churches merged and relocated in a new building known as Faith United Church of Christ. Two of the beautiful stained-glass windows from the former churches were brought to the new building. In 1983, the church was able to move the bell, which had been a part of the original St. Joseph Post Office, to the current location. In 2001, the cornerstones of the three churches were placed at the front entrance of the church, which is now a nondenominational community church.

Mt. Hulda Lutheran Church, Cole Camp

Located in Cole Camp, Mt. Hulda sits high on a hilltop south of the town. The third church building on the site, it is built of natural stone and was dedicated in 1953. This congregation is active and has several events throughout the year, including a live nativity display, annual fish fry, and a church float in many of the local Christmas parades. In the early years of the fish fry, congregation members caught the fish and cooked them in iron kettles over open fires. With the growth in numbers of people attending the event, the fish are now purchased from markets and cooked in gas fryers.

Believers Bible Chapel, Union

Believers Bible Chapel in Union started as two families, the Phil Smith family and the Lou Gettings family. A year later, three more families joined them. This group met together for Bible studies, especially the scriptures concerning the New Testament Church. The group continued to grow and, in 1977, they bought land and began building a church. The church was finished in stages to accommodate congregational growth. The entire church was dedicated on December 11, 1983.

United Church of Christ, Columbia

In 1921, a group of faculty, students, and Columbia residents of German Evangelical background started the Evangelical Club, and by 1932, the first church building, The Chapel, was constructed on Hitt Street. In the early 1960s, the Evangelical and Reformed Church joined with the Congregational Christian Church to become the United Church of Christ.

The Chapel was getting crowded and was seriously damaged by fire in December 1965. The congregation bought five acres west of town. The current building was completed and dedicated in September 1969 as Columbia United Church of Christ. An education wing was added in 1998.

St. Margaret of Antioch Catholic Church, Osage Bend

On February 25, 1907, the first meeting to organize and build a Catholic church in Osage Bend was held. Up until this time, families had to travel to nearby towns. Occasionally, a priest would come to Osage Bend and families would gather for a service in the home of John and Margaret Sommer. There were twenty-three families at the organizational meeting. After the meeting, Henry Bode and Herman Sommer went to St. Louis and petitioned Archbishop Glennon for permission to build a new Catholic church and asked that he send a priest. The archbishop granted permission and said he would send a priest if the community could provide $600 a year for a salary. Joseph and Caroline (Roth) Hofer donated the land, and construction began by local families with the Bode brothers leading.

The church was a framed, tin-clad structure with a tall steeple and belfry. The two side altars and the main altar were hand carved by the Bode brothers. The original pastor, Father Peter Wigger, celebrated the first mass on November 1, 1907.

In 1957, plans were drawn for a new church building, and on May 8, 1957, demolition of the first church began. This building, which is the current building, was constructed of red brick. It was completed on September 28, 1957. The building is of modern design. Its ceiling was constructed of wood beams with the beams extending from the floor up. The tower at the back of the church holds the bell from the first church.

Remodeling of the church took place in 1979 and included a reconciliation room, giving parishioners the choice of having a face-to-face confessional or sitting behind a curtain. The altar was replaced and paneling added in the sanctuary. Windows on the west side of the sanctuary were all destroyed in a storm on May 3, 2003. Since then, new stained-glass windows have been added on both sides of the church.

First Baptist Church, Raytown

Raytown First Baptist began as a home church with sixteen people from Virginia, Kentucky, Tennessee, and the Carolinas on December 10, 1842. It was organized as the West Fork of the Little Blue Church and was welcomed into the Blue River Baptist Association in July 1843. The first pastor was the Reverend Jeremiah Farmer. The first building was built of stone in 1846 and was contracted by Daniel and Morgan Boone, grandsons of Daniel Boone.

In 1859, a larger structure was built at the same location. With the exception of four years during the Civil War, the congregation worshipped in this building until 1897. By 1951 it was time for a new building, which was built across the street from the previous location on Blue Ridge Boulevard. In the 1960s, the church built a new auditorium and changed its name to First Baptist Church of Raytown. The fifth sanctuary was built in 1964, and ten years later, the Fellowship Hall and Sunday school rooms were constructed. The church constructed the current building in 1999 between 350 Highway and Seventy-fifth Street. In 2006 the membership was almost eight thousand.

James River Assembly of God, Ozark

James River Assembly is a large church with a small church feel. It grew from its original four families in a storefront church to a megachurch that seats three thousand.

James River Assembly is just outside of Springfield, at the Ozark exit on Highway CC. This church has grown tremendously since its beginning. It has a separate youth building as well as the equipment to put on concerts complete with light shows.

The church has its own Christian bookstore inside and is also equipped with a Starbuck's coffee shop. James River puts on several events during the year including a citywide "I Love America" fireworks display in Springfield. Those who worship here have many opportunities to get involved in ministries, which include kids' ministries, student ministries, and adult ministries ranging from Bible Fellowship to Jamesriverwomen.

This modern church offers an upbeat service for today's Christians.

Harper Chapel, Osage Beach

Harper Chapel in Osage Beach began with a Methodist class led by Thomas Ezard in 1868. The class met in homes until it became too large, at which time it moved to the local school. In 1912, the first cement building was constructed. Mounting steps—built to assist ladies in long skirts as they climbed into and out of wagons—are still on the grounds today.

The church expanded in 1962; the first service was March 10, 1963, and was led by the Reverend George Ryder. There were several building additions over the years with the most recent in 2004. One of the highlights of this addition was that the original cement building was developed into a small chapel.

Immaculate Conception
Catholic Church, Springfield

There was a need for a Catholic church in Springfield, so Reverend Francis W. Graham was sent to be the first pastor to the 110 Catholics in the area. The first service was held in Phelps's Hall downtown. In 1874, property was purchased on the northeast corner of Tampa and Campbell. Ten years later, a massive red brick Gothic church was built. The church bell weighed more than a ton and was used to signal the call to worship for many years.

The old building, the oldest Catholic church in southwest Missouri, was torn down in 1957; the new church was built at Cherokee and Fremont. The first mass in this building was held August 3, 1958. The church continued to grow, and in 1973, the current fifteen-acre site was purchased on South Fremont Street. Groundbreaking took place in 1979, and the church was dedicated on August 31, 1981.

There have been several additions to the church since 1981. The current campus includes the church building, educational facilities, a gym, cafeteria, priest's residence, grotto, library, media center, and fine arts center. As of 2004, more than thirteen hundred families were members of Immaculate Conception.

Cathedral of St. Joseph, Jefferson City

St. Joseph Parish began April 6, 1958, when the first bishop of the Jefferson City Diocese, Bishop Joseph M. Marling announced the formation of a third parish in Jefferson City. Because of overcrowding at St. Peter's Cathedral located next to the state capitol and to better serve the growing Catholic community it was decided to construct a new parish on a nineteen-acre site located on the west side of the city. The first red brick building constructed housed a cafeteria, church, and six classrooms for the parish of 250 families. Father Kenneth McDonnell served as the first pastor.

Two additional buildings were constructed for the rectory and a convent. The convent housed the Sisters of Mercy who had been recruited from Ireland by the second pastor, the Reverend Monsignor Francis O'Duignan.

Monsignor Gerard Poelker was installed September 10, 1964, as the third pastor of St. Joseph's. It was during this tenure in 1966 that plans were made to build a modern, circular Cathedral. On August 20, 1967, Bishop Marling and Monsignor Poelker presided over the groundbreaking ceremony. By the time that the first mass was celebrated by Bishop Marling at midnight on Christmas 1968, the parish had grown to 650 families.

On August 18, 1969, Bishop Michael F. McAuliffe was ordained and installed as the second bishop of the Diocese of Jefferson City following the retirement of Bishop Joseph Marling. The following year, St. Joseph Parish was elevated to the title of the Cathedral of Saint Joseph.

In 1966 plans were made for the modern circular church. Groundbreaking took place in 1967. The entire diocese contributed to its new cathedral both financially and spiritually. Upon its completion, the original church was remodeled into classrooms for the parish school. The pipe organ in the church was constructed by the Wicks Organ Company of Highland, Illinois, in 1969.

Currently, the cathedral parish serves 4,200 parishioners in 1,397 households and the Cathedral school has an enrollment of 470 students. The parish community and school continue to grow.

The diocese was formed from territory taken from the Archdiocese of St. Louis, the Diocese of Kansas City, and the Diocese of Saint Joseph. The diocese consists of thirty-eight counties in mainly rural northern and central Missouri, and includes the urban areas of Columbia, and the state capital, Jefferson City.

The diocese has ninety-five parishes, fifteen missions, sixty-eight active diocesan priests, eight religious priests, and eighty-eight thousand Catholics. It has seventy-three women religious, two religious brothers, and forty-three permanent deacons.

Iglesia de Dios, Sedalia

This church, which translates to "Church of God," is one of a growing number in Missouri catering to the state's increasing Hispanic population. It is located in a brick storefront in Sedalia's historic downtown and is painted in bright red.

Many traditional Sedalia churches have welcomed Hispanics to their services by posting signs in the church yard reading "Todos bienvenidos con la familia de Dios," meaning "all are welcome with the family of God."

Miracle Deliverance Holiness Church, Anderson

As new congregations develop in Missouri they frequently use old storefronts in the downtown areas of small towns as their church. One such ministry is the Miracle Deliverance Holiness Church located in Anderson in extreme southwest Missouri.

Chapter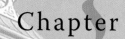

SYMBOLS OF OUR FAITH

Lord and Savior
On Your throne
Wash my past
And take me home

Did you hold the holder of my burdens-
Crossbeam of the Cross?
Was it on you that Christ died
So I would not suffer loss?

The nail pierced hands and feet
Melded to your cumbersome frame?
Dear salvation immensely purchased
Free when asked in Jesus name.

—LCK 2006

*M*issouri is rich in symbolic features, from windows in a church that tell a story or honor a saint, to statues of people or monuments like the praying hands that remind us of our faith and strong religious beliefs. Overlooking almost every town is a tall church spire that can be seen for miles. Reminders such as these move our thoughts and hearts to God and help us to keep our focus on him when the struggles of everyday life get us down. When our faith is weak or we are overwhelmed with things in life, we can look to these symbols for comfort, inspiration, and encouragement.

St. Joseph Catholic Church, Westphalia

The small German town that sits off of Highway 63 in central Missouri demands attention. The scene is breathtaking. This village on the hill is crowned with the magnificent view of St. Joseph Catholic Church that can be seen from anywhere in town. Father Ferdinand Helias came to central Missouri in 1838 and founded the town and several churches in the area, serving a large population of German settlers.

When Father Helias established his first churches he settled them with citizens who were German but also from one of the many city-states that formed the country in the early 1800s. Settlers from the Westphalia and Hanover regions settled in Westphalia. Rhinelanders settled in Loose Creek. Rich Fountain on the Gasconade River became home to the Bavarians, while Low Germans from Belgium and Hanover moved into what became Taos. In this manner Father Helias kept the peace among the many rival groups that did not always get along.

So beautiful is St. Joseph Church in Westphalia that it was once described in a poem as the "Pearl of Osage County." Its architecture is prominently featured in "The Arts and Architecture of German Settlements in Missouri." While separating the German people kept the peace, it did not completely end the rivalries. St. Joseph underwent a remodeling in 1905 to raise the ceilings after it was discovered that those at Sacred Heart Church in the rival Bavarian town of Rich Fountain were higher. A second balcony also was added at that time. The steeple of the church, which dominates the skyline, was added in 1848, thirty-five years after the church was constructed.

Sacred Heart, Rich Fountain

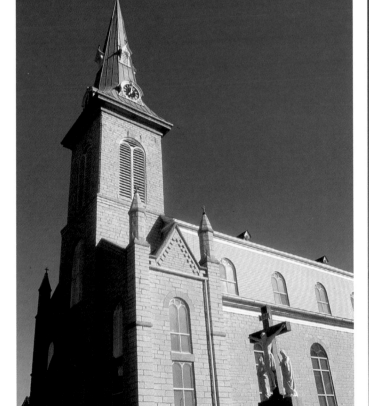

Locust Grove United Methodist Church, Midway

This church, which was started by Reuben Hatton who migrated west through St. Louis, has been serving the community just west of Columbia without interruption since 1817. Midway United Methodist met in homes for thirteen years until a brick chapel was built. The chapel was replaced in 1870 with a new building, and the name of the church was changed. *Locust* was added in recognition of the locust trees that had been planted in the area.

Among the church's activities are an annual country dinner and bazaar, vacation Bible school, and mission trips. Around two hundred members continue to lead in the support of Methodism in Missouri. The picture here shows a window in the church reflecting the dawning of a new day.

St. Francis Xavier Catholic Church, Taos

It was in the summer of 1838 that the saintly Father Helias came to central Missouri to care for the souls of the German immigrants. Only twenty families comprised the congregation, when mass was first said on May 28, 1838.

Shortly after, ten acres of land was purchased from Henry and Gertrude Haar for $5 to be used for a church and school. The year 1840 saw the erection of the first church, a rather crude and simple log structure dedicated to St. Francis Xavier, a fa-

mous Jesuit missionary to India. The site of the Parish was named Haarville. It was so called for many years; but when some soldiers who had fought in the Battle of Taos and Sacramento came back from the war with Mexico, the town was forever referred to as Taos.

On April 6, 1844, the cornerstone of the second church was laid, which would claim the distinction of being the first stone house of worship to be built in the interior of the state of Missouri. More than a year lapsed before the new edifice was ready for occupancy.

In 1842, Father Helias transferred his residence from New Westphalia to Taos, and from that year until his death he lived amongst the people he loved, and whom he served so faithfully for so many years. On the morning of August 11, 1874, the "Apostle of Central Missouri" was found lying in the yard near the church—a stroke had ended his life. He was buried in the little cemetery in Taos where he remained until 1964. On February 29 of that year, he was reburied in the church. A museum in the church basement displays many Father Helias artifacts including his cast iron coffin and vestments, in addition to historic items such as wooden shoes from the town.

Under the pastorate of the Reverend John Gruender, in 1881 plans were made for the erection of a new church, the old rock church having become too small to house the congregation. This was the third church to be built in Taos, and still stands firm and solid today, a tribute to the zeal and faith of the people at the time. With the exception of improvements, church furnishings, modifications, and beautification, the present church is the same as it was in 1883, the year in which it was dedicated to the honor and glory of God.

One highlight of the church is its three masterpieces. The oil paintings, housed in the three altars, are the work of the Italian Baroque-era artist Guido Reni (1575–1642). These three paintings are dated 1601. These paintings were a gift from Father Helias' mother who was the Countess of Lens. The superior general of the Jesuit order brought them to this country from Europe in 1846. The central altar is adorned with a work entitled *The Flagellation*, which is shown here. On the left side altar is a painting of St. Francis Xavier, the parish patron. The right side altar houses the painting of St. Francis of Assisi, one of the most beloved saints. The financial contributions of parishioners made it possible for Tom Sater of Sater Restorations, St. Louis, to restore these paintings during the 1998 restoration of the church.

Other works of art can be found in the church's Stations of the Cross, which are oil paintings dated to 1887 and also restored after being found stored in the church basement.

Yeager Union Church, Edmonson

This small rural church in Edmonson, near Lincoln, is a nondenominational church that sits high on a hill overlooking the Lake of the Ozarks. It

was started in 1853 and was built by Solomon Yeager. A cemetery lies next to the church and holds the unmarked graves of many pioneers and American Indians, along with the graves of eighteen American veterans. A flagpole was erected to honor these vets.

In the early 1900s, the congregation began to deteriorate and the building fell into disarray. In 1953, members of the community came together to repair the building, adding a fellowship hall. Services were held in the old building until 1977 when the church closed again. It reopened in 1982 and has held services since that time. In 2005, a kitchen, bathrooms, library space, and a multipurpose area were added, bringing running water to the building for the first time.

St. Michael Catholic Church, Steelville

A statue of St. Michael greets visitors to this tourist town deep in the Missouri Ozarks. He is depicted in his role as the field commander of the army of God. The little church is home away from home to many campers and floaters who vacation in Steelville, the float capital of Missouri.

Sacred Heart Catholic Church, Sedalia

A group of German-speaking Catholics established Sacred Heart Parish in Sedalia in March 1882. The first church, school, and convent were dedicated October 1, 1882. A new church building was constructed with the new cornerstone being placed in May 8, 1892. The church has grown over the years, requiring a new school in 1907 and a new convent in 1909. It is one of the finest examples of Gothic architecture in Sedalia. Recent restoration projects have included refinishing the sanctuary including all three altars, the statuary, the walls, ceilings and flooring. Much of the color, gold leaf, and ornate woodwork that was removed or painted over has been restored.

Midvale Pentecostal Holiness Church, Summersville

You can see many marquee-type signs outside churches bearing reminders of service times and church information, but many also give community members thoughts to ponder and encouragement to live life outside of the church as they do inside the church. Following is a picture of such a sign, posted outside of Midvale Pentecostal Holiness Church located five miles north of Summersville. A large photo mural of a natural scene adorns the inside of the church.

Harmony (Harmonie) Church, Warren County

Harmonie Church was the first Lutheran Evangelical Church in Warren County and has largely mothered and fostered the growth of the surrounding Evangelical churches. The churches in Wright City, Warrenton, Steinhagen, and Lippstadt owe their growth and development, at least in part, to Harmonie Church.

The church can trace its history to sometime around 1842–43 when Reverend Herman Garlicks from Femme Osage would ride his horse the thirteen miles to Harmonie on the Upper Charrette River to shepherd the flock of God. The earliest exact record was a baptism on September 3, 1843. Most of the names are lost, but in the ensuing years there were 861 baptisms and 246 marriages performed at Harmonie.

Harmonie flourished for forty years under the watchful care of Pastor Karl Strack. His influence was such that the church was commonly called "Strack Church." At its height under Pastor Strack, sixty-eight families called Harmonie home.

For reasons unknown, Harmonie was closed to regular worship services from 1932 to 1996. However, in 1941 the church and adjoining cemetery were incorporated and the Charrette Memorial Association was formed. The organization consisted of a nine-member board with Joe Stevenson as president, William H. Wehrman as secretary, and Edmund Hollenbeck as treasurer. It was because of their great love for the church and their desire to preserve its link to the past that today both a religious site and a hallowed burial place still exist.

On February 10, 1990, tragedy struck when Harmonie Church burned to the ground. Everything was ash. Even her bell was nothing but molten metal.

But God had not forgotten Harmonie. Hosts of people were stirred to rebuild Harmonie Church. A community chapel association was formed with Lola Baseel, Roger Beckmeyer, Ed Boyce, Earl Neely, Carol Wolfe, Rick Klenke, and Al Ledebuhr, who served as president. They found that the exact dimensions of the original church were on record so an historical reproduction would be possible. Countless people came armed with hammers and paintbrushes. They gave money and time, offered their skills, prayers, labor, love, encouragement, and sympathetic understanding when problems arose.

From the ashes a new church arose. After 150 years, Harmony (Harmonie) Church stands amidst her forest of trees. The vaulted ceiling still affords acoustical perfection. The elevated pulpit is gone but some of the other furniture is a link to the past. Mrs. Hollenbeck was storing the pulpit chairs at the time of the fire and returned them to the new church. They were refinished by Kurt Nathan as a gift to the church.

Beginning Memorial Day Sunday in 1991, Harmony began to hold a regular schedule of multi-denominational services. As the Innsbruck Village continued to grow and more permanent, year-round homes were being built, Harmony's attendance swelled and the idea of holding weekly services began to surface. In 1991 the board invited Reverend Richard Perkins to accept the role of pastor. He accepted and continues to serve the congregation.

On Palm Sunday 1996, Harmony Church began to hold services on the Lord's Day. It had been almost sixty-five years since this "church in the wild woods" met on a weekly schedule. Harmony today has more than seventy families that attend services and the record of financial support and participation is outstanding.

Again let us say, "Kommt Laset Uns Anbeten (Come Let us Worship)."

St. Peter Catholic Church, Jefferson City

The history of St. Peter Church and Catholicism in Jefferson City can be traced back to just ten years after the founding of the capital city in 1821. Father Felix L. Verreydt celebrated the first recorded Mass in Jefferson City in 1831 in the home of Bernard Upschulte. In 1838, Father Ferdinand Helias organized the local Catholics into a community and celebrated Mass in private homes until a site could be selected for a church. His original candlesticks and crucifix that he carried in his saddlebags throughout his ministry are on display in the St. Peter Parish Life Center.

The first site for St. Peter Parish Church was the old state capitol building. A petition was presented to the General Assembly to allow local Catholics to purchase the building as the first church. The governor and the Senate approved, but the measure failed the House of Representatives by four votes. The first Catholic Church in Jefferson City was then constructed in 1845 to 1846, under Father Helias, on the present site of St. Peter School. The structure was a thirty-by-twenty-two-foot oaken-board building. Father Helias named the new church building in honor of St. Ignatius Loyola, the founder of the Jesuits.

The Jesuits soon turned the care of the new mission over to Archbishop Peter R. Kenrick, St. Louis, and in 1846 the Archbishop named Father James S. Murphy the first resident pastor. When Father Murphy dedicated the new church, he named it in honor of St. Peter. The young church served the community well for twelve years until the growth of the Catholic population forced Father William Walsh, the fourth pastor, to construct the second St. Peter church structure on the corner of Broadway and High Streets. It was built of brick and dedicated in 1856 on a plot of land purchased for $600.

The brick church served its function until 1881 when it was razed to make way for the present church.

The present church was constructed with 800,000 bricks donated by G. H. Dulle. It is 173.5 feet in length. It is 60 feet in width. It has a seating capacity of seven hundred. The clock tower, a city landmark, rises to a height of 170 feet. The tower contains four bells cast by the Struckstede Foundry with an aggregate weight of eight thousand pounds, purchased at a cost of $1,354 and dedicated to St. Peter (fifty-five inches in diameter), St. Joseph (forty-six inches), The Sacred Heart of Jesus (thirty-four inches) and The Blessed Virgin Mary (twenty-eight inches).

It is impossible to separate the parish history from the history of Jefferson City and the city's role as the seat of state government. The clock, installed in 1888, is of service to both church and state. It rings the hour for divine services and every four years the new governor of Missouri is sworn into office when its C-sharp minor cords have struck noon. Governor Joseph P. Teasdale was a member of St. Peter and attended noon Mass frequently.

In 1956, Missouri was divided into four dioceses, and the Diocese of Jefferson City was formed. St. Peter Church was selected as the first cathedral. The Cathedral of St. Peter served the founding bishop, the Most Reverend Joseph M. Marling, C.PP.S., for twelve years, from his installation in 1956 until Christmas Eve 1968 when the cathedral's jurisdiction was transferred to St. Joseph Parish.

Seven years after the parish began, St. Peter School was founded. A noteworthy Missourian to attend St. Peter School as a child was former governor James T. Blair, who served as the state's chief executive from 1957 to 1961.

St. Peter School has the distinction of being the "Ninth Capitol of Missouri." After fire destroyed the Capitol building in 1911, Monsignor Selinger offered the use of the school to the state without charge. The House of Representatives accepted his proposal and the remainder of the Forty-sixth General Assembly was conducted at the school.

In 1931, St. Peter High School was started and, shortly thereafter, the Christian Brothers arrived. The high school served until the founding of Helias Interparish High School in 1955.

Presbyterian Church, Hollister

In 1912, several small Presbyterian groups in the Hollister area that had met in homes for services came together to build a church where they could worship. The cornerstone was laid in 1915. The church is commonly referred to as, "The Church on the Hill."

Earl Gibson and his father made the pulpit that is still used today in the church. Earl also was the one who delivered the church bell from the river landing, carting it to the church site with mule and hack. The bell was ordered from Montgomery Ward in Chicago and still rings every Sunday to call the community to worship.

Historical Christ Episcopal Church, Springfield

This congregation worships in the oldest church building in Springfield, located at 601 East Walnut. The stained-glass windows date back to 1870 and the stone chancel dates back to 1927. This building is a beautiful display of ecclesiastical Gothic architecture. Included here are some pictures that show the architecture and the beauty of the glorious stained-glass window.

Assemblies of God Headquarters, Springfield

The General Council of the Assemblies of God is located in Springfield, occupying ten city blocks with eighteen buildings. The story of how the church formed is fascinating.

In 1913, a woman named Rachel Sizelove came to Springfield to visit family. While in prayer one day, she saw a vision of a sparkling fountain in the heart of Springfield. The fountain sprang up gradually and begin to flow to the east, west, north, and south until soon living water covered the entire land. A short time later, in 1914, the General Council of the Assemblies of God formed in Hot Springs, Arkansas. A small headquarters and print operations were set up in Findley, Ohio. Then, in 1915, the operation moved to St. Louis, where it remained until 1918, when it relocated to a building on Pacific Street in Springfield.

Today the sprawling campus is home to Gospel Publishing House, Assembly of God World Missions, the Plower Pentecostal Heritage Center, and a museum. Visitors can enjoy the beauty of the campus. A chapel in the building hosts daily services for employees. Stained-glass windows accent the chapel.

Two years after the church's founding, the pioneers of the Assemblies of God adopted sixteen beliefs for the Fellowship. This *Statement of Fundamental Truths* remains virtually unchanged. Four of these beliefs are considered the major tenets of the Fellowship and are portrayed in the magnificent artwork of Ron DiCianni in the lobby of the Assemblies of God National Headquarters. They include *Salvation through Jesus Christ, Divine Healing for the Sick, Baptism in the Holy Spirit, and The Second Coming of Christ.*

St. Paul Episcopal Church, Ironton

Located in Ironton, this church was organized in 1869 and has held services continuously since that time. Judge Emerson donated the land and the building plans. The community, including non-members, participated in constructing the present building with donations, labor, and materials. The building was finished in 1870, and the first service was held on Christmas Eve. The style of the church is Wood Gothic and has remained essentially unchanged. The steeply sloped roof is covered with cypress shingles, which are painted in a diagonal pattern. The windows are period stained-glass and the original pews are walnut.

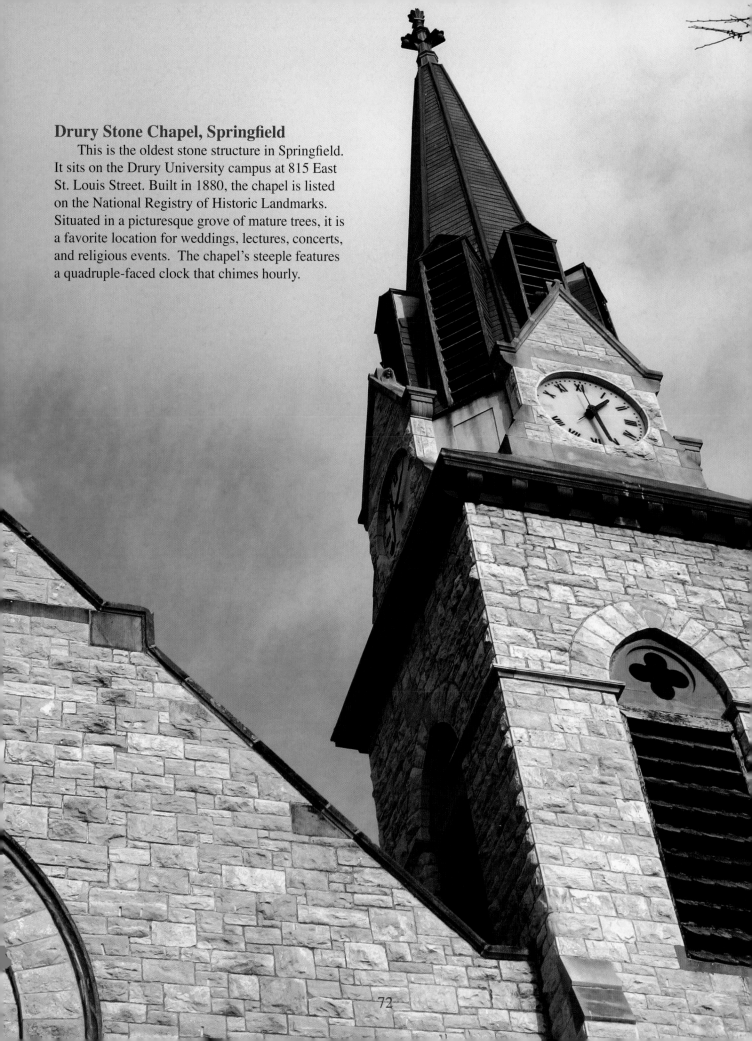

Drury Stone Chapel, Springfield

This is the oldest stone structure in Springfield. It sits on the Drury University campus at 815 East St. Louis Street. Built in 1880, the chapel is listed on the National Registry of Historic Landmarks. Situated in a picturesque grove of mature trees, it is a favorite location for weddings, lectures, concerts, and religious events. The chapel's steeple features a quadruple-faced clock that chimes hourly.

St. Joseph's Chapel, Ursuline Academy, Arcadia

Built in Arcadia in 1907, this chapel—noted for its beautiful stained glass windows—is located on the grounds of the Ursuline Academy, which was started by the Reverend Jerry C. Berryman in 1846 as a Methodist high school. From 1861 to 1864, the academy served as a Union Army hospital. The Ursuline Order of nuns bought the academy in 1877 and turned it into a boarding school for women. At its peak, more than one hundred young women from across the world attended. The last class graduated in 1970, and the campus served as a convent until 1985 when the order was moved to St. Louis. No church services have been held in the chapel since. Now under private ownership, the academy is listed as a historic area and is available for tours and other functions.

Shrine of St. Joseph, St. Louis

This historic and religious landmark in St. Louis was founded in 1844. It has an exquisitely detailed ceiling and a stunning main altar. Many visitors are awestruck by the beauty of the Shrine. There are more than thirty hand-carved wooden statues and other one-of-a-kind religious works of art that portray old-world craftsmanship. In the 1970s when the Shrine was in danger of being torn town and was in poor condition, a group came together naming themselves the Friends of the Shrine. For more than twenty-five years, the Friends have made a successful effort to save and restore this edifice to its former grandeur.

The Shrine is often referred to as "The Church of Miracles." It is the site of the only Vatican-authenticated miracle in the Midwest. In 1867, the parishioners vowed to build a monument to St. Joseph if they were spared from the cholera epidemic. All who signed the vow were spared, and a fifty-foot-high Italian-Renaissance main altar called the Altar of Answered Prayers was erected.

St. Vincent De Paul Church, St. Mary's of the Barrens Church, and the National Shrine of Our Lady of the Miraculous Medal, Perryville

A small log building on Sycamore Lane served as the first chapel for Catholics who came to Perryville from Barrens County, Kentucky. It was built and blessed in 1812 by Vicar General James Maxwell, pastor at Ste. Genevieve.

Prior to this, Mass was occasionally said at the home of Joseph Tucker. A couple of years later Father Marie Joseph Dunand, a Trappist monk, started visiting the area a few times a year and he suggested that the people ask Bishop Dubourg to choose Perryville as the site of the diocesan seminary.

The bishop established Saint Mary's of the Barrens in the fall of 1818. St. Mary's of the Barrens Church soon outgrew the original log structure and in 1826 construction began on a larger church that took ten years to complete and served both English and French immigrants. The church that was originally Tuscan was built with limestone quarried on the property. The church soon became known as the Church of the Assumption because of the painting of the *Assumption of the Blessed Virgin Mary* located behind the main altar. This was also the first permanent settlement of Vincentian priests and brothers in the Western Hemisphere and the first seminary in the Louisiana Territory.

In 1913 renovations were made and the front of the church was changed to Romanesque-style architecture. The original towers on either side of the front door were removed and a vestibule added. A window that was made in Munich, Germany, was placed on the front wall; the ornamental rose stained-glass window is a portrayal of *The Madonna of the Chair* by Raphael.

The Shrine of our Lady of the Miraculous Medal was added in 1928 to the south side of the church. The niche behind the statue of Mary is inlaid with gold mosaics and the interior walls are lined with panels of rosatto marble. Roman arches accent the interior and there are two 45-foot domes and seven small chapels on the north and south walls. Paintings and frescoes in the church were restored in 1948 and a freestanding Angelus Bell Tower, designed to match the church's façade, was built in 1980.

St. Boniface Parish was built in 1868 when German-speaking Catholics of the area asked the Most Rev. T. R. Kendrick, Archbishop of St. Louis, for a church to be built where they could receive sermons and instruction in German. In 1947, St. Boniface Parish and Assumption Parish combined. When the cornerstone was laid for the new church in 1964, the parish became St. Vincent de Paul Parish. The old St. Boniface Church was razed. Two stained-glass windows representing each church can be seen inside.

St. Mary's of the Barrens Church became a Marian Shrine, the National Shrine of our Lady of the Miraculous Medal, and the Vincentian Community Chapel. The National Shrine of Our Lady of the Miraculous Medal has been placed on the National Register of Historic Places. It is open to visitors and is a peaceful place to spend some time.

Grace Episcopal Church, Chillicothe

This church has been in existence in Chillicothe since 1870. The building is in the Gothic Revival style. The interior reflects the Victorian era and is designed in the form of a typical English country church. The church and the parish hall are made entirely of wood. The windows are stained and painted glass. Some date back to the 1870s and the newest ones were installed in 1911. The structure is an example of early prefabricated construction, the major parts being built in St. Louis and brought to the site by riverboat and wagon. The church was consecrated on May 11, 1876.

The pipe organ in the church was installed the same year and still provides music for the congregation. The church has never been without a congregation and it has been a place of prayer and worship since it was constructed.

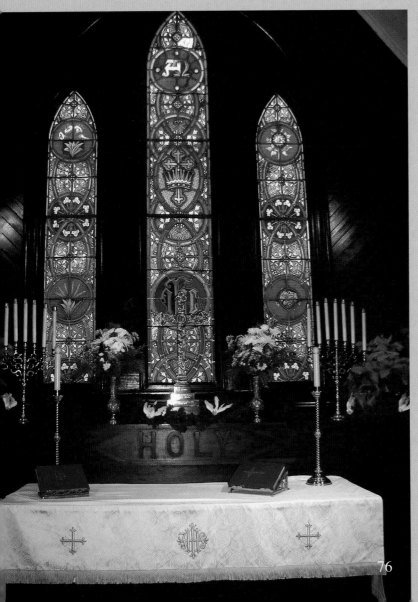

76

Grace Presbyterian Church, Crystal City

This rock church in Crystal City was originally an Episcopal church, built in 1891 by the Crystal Plate Glass Company as a place for their workers to worship. Land beside the church was landscaped for a beautiful park, which also includes a fountain. In 1926, the church was given to the congregation and the name was changed to Grace Presbyterian Church. In one of the pictures you will see two stone guard towers. They were erected so that the payroll for the glass company workers could be protected. When it arrived on the train and other ways, there would be a guard in each tower with guns to make sure the money got to the bank, which also was across the street from the church.

St. Mary's Catholic Church, Glasgow

Glasgow is a Missouri River town settled by Southerners in 1836. Following the Civil War, the town began to change as railroads replaced steamboats for transportation and Irish immigrants moved to the town to work on the rail lines. The Irish and also German transplants brought their Catholic faith with them, establishing St. Mary's Church in 1869. The church building contains many beautiful examples of stained glass and statuary.

United Methodist Church, Rocheport

You don't have to be inside to enjoy the splendor of the windows at Rocheport's United Methodist Church. They are just as beautiful from the outside. The church was built in 1901, although it was established much earlier in 1835.

St. Joseph Catholic Church, Edina

St. Joseph can trace its roots back to the pioneer settlement days of Edina. By 1837, Roman Catholics began to settle in Knox County. In June of 1843, Father Thomas Cusack, who served the churches in New London, St. Paul, Indian Creek, Brush Creek, Hunnewell, and St. Patrick, made a visit to Edina to celebrate the first recorded mass here. The building of the present church began in 1872. Built under the direction of Louis Weishar, the church was dedicated by Bishop Ryan on October 10, 1875. Several notable additions to the church came in the following years. In 1885, a pipe organ, which was reportedly produced for the Centennial Celebration of the United States, was purchased and arrived in Edina on three train cars. At the time, this organ was said to be the largest pipe organ west of the Mississippi River. In 1890, the church steeple was completed, and three bells were added to it in 1900. More additions came in 1920 when seventeen more stained-glass windows, the marble sanctuary floor and communion rail, and the steeple clock were installed. This beautiful old church built in 1874 is a towering beacon leading all to town with its 175-foot belfry.

Cave Springs Memorial Church, Willard

The simple bell tower stands above this church in Cave Springs, a small spot in the road north of Willard. It was formerly Mt. Zion Presbyterian Church, but when the structure was no longer needed, the Cave Springs community wanted to save it. They purchased it and named it Cave Springs Memorial Church. Services are held in the building a couple times a year and an egg roast is held on Palm Sunday.

Praying Hands Memorial, Webb City

The hands remain forever folded on a mound overlooking the city. American flags flap around the silent memorial, and carved in stone in front of the statue are six simple words: "Hands in prayer. World in peace."

The sight of Praying Hands Memorial in Webb City leaves a lasting impression. Each year, thousands of visitors and locals see the giant hands.

The memorial started in 1970, when a twenty-year-old student named Jack Dawson approached the Webb City Park Board and the Historical Society about an art piece he wished to build in the city's King Jack Park. The organizations quickly approved the statue and encouraged local citizens and merchants to help fund the project.

Dawson began the work in his own backyard by creating a steel understructure covered with a metal lath. Curious locals said the sight resembled a gigantic birdcage. When the steelwork was ready for the white stucco covering in the fall of 1972, the hands were taken to a mound in the park, near Highway 71.

On April 28, 1974, the thirty-two-foot, one-hundred-ton memorial opened to the public at a dedication ceremony. That day, the hand's creator said, "The hands symbolize the need for a personal commitment and relationship to God."

More than thirty years later, Praying Hands Memorial remains a symbol of the artist's faith and the importance of prayer. Admission to the memorial, which is open to visitors year-round, is free. To visit Praying Hands Memorial, take Highway 71 to the eastern edge of Webb City.

St. Thomas the Apostle Catholic Church, St. Thomas

Since 1919, residents of St. Thomas haven't needed their wristwatches. The four-faced clock housed in a tower high above St. Thomas the Apostle Church chimes every quarter hour, keeping this town and its citizens on time for mass and other activities. All four clocks are run by one mechanism that keeps them in sync. A pendulum regulates the clock mechanism housed inside the bell tower, while cast-iron weights provide the power to keep it running. This cast-iron frame measures two by three feet and is packed with gears, springs, and levers, closely resembling a much smaller movement that would be found inside a mantel clock. A member of the church is assigned the duty of upkeep on the clock, which usually consists of keeping it oiled.

When the present church building was built in 1883, the clock was not part of it. It was added in 1919. Gerhard Bersmeyer donated the clock in honor of his son, Henry, who died in World War I.

A marvel of engineering, the movement regulates the four clock faces and strikes the four bells located thirty feet above it. The bronze bells were cast in St. Louis in 1895 and donated as memorials by parishioners.

Prior to 1948, the spire on top of the steeple was much higher. On the evening of May 1, 1948, a tornado struck St. Thomas causing major damage. The entire church steeple was blown down, causing much damage to the windows, the church interior and the roof. Also major damage was done to other buildings on the church property, which included two schools, the convent and the rectory. Parishioners were unable to repair the school buildings, but were successful in repairing all of the other buildings including the church. However, the spire that was replaced on the steeple is significantly shorter in height than the original.

A photo in the back of church shows the clock movement buried in the rubble. The clock was repaired and has run ever since, although the hands have to be deiced from time to time following winter storms. This church is another one established in central Missouri by Father Helias.

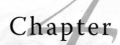

Chapter 4

PEOPLE OF FAITH

Heavenly Father
Thank you for sending Your Son
Forgive my sins
Make my heart pure

You sacrificed Your only Son
His blood was shed on the cross
He was persecuted and died
All to make my eternity sure

You had to turn away
Jesus heaped with my sin
Your love remained strong
It was sin's only cure
—LCK

*M*any people have contributed to the deep religious roots of Missouri. This section includes a look at just a few who made a significant contribution to the development of Missouri's faith. Most of these stories were taken from the pages of *Rural Missouri*.

Father Helias

Ferdinand Benedict Mary Guislan Helias D'Huddghem—better known as Father Helias—was born into a royal family in the Flanders region of Belgium in 1796. His could have been a life of luxury. Instead, he traveled to the new world with the intention of setting up schools for American Indians. His plans changed when he arrived in Missouri.

Father Helias would become known as the "Apostle of Central Missouri" for his work in bringing the Catholic faith to the German settlers here. He laid the foundation for seven churches, in Westphalia, St. Thomas, Loose Creek, Jefferson City, Rich Fountain, Cedron, and Taos, in just seven years. A true diplomat, he recognized that the German settlers were from different regions and did not always get along.

"They were all German, they were all Catholic . . . but they were Bavarians and Rhinelanders and Westphalians. They were from three different kingdoms of Germany and therefore they couldn't get along," Helias wrote. So each parish served a distinct ethnic group.

Hardship and peril followed Father Helias as he traveled central Missouri by horseback, delivering sermons, hearing confessions and performing weddings and baptisms. He nearly drowned several times and was shot at during the Civil War.

All of the parishes he founded with the exception of Assumption in Cedron are thriving today, each with its own parish school. Life in the towns revolves around the church and school, a lasting tribute to Father Helias. In addition, the Diocese of Jefferson City named its high school in Jefferson City in his honor.

But the real tribute to his hard work can be found in the fact that Cole and Osage Counties, where most of his churches were established, remain the most-Catholic of any Missouri region. From his humble beginnings dozens of new parishes sprung up and remain active.

Father Helias died in 1874. Jesuit customs required him to be buried in St. Louis, despite his wish to remain in his beloved Taos. But while a group of men held vigil in the night, they were frightened by a loud report that sounded like a gunshot. The glass window in his coffin had shattered. Missouri Pacific Railroad officials refused to carry the coffin because its seal was broken. The parishioners had no choice but to bury him in the St. Francis Xavier cemetery. He was later reburied in a tomb at the back of the church. A museum in the church basement displays his cast iron coffin and the shards of broken glass, along with many items from his time in Missouri including his Bible and the vestments in which he was buried.

Father Moses Berry, Ash Grove

Father Moses Berry was born and raised in the Ash Grove area, a generation that had been preceded by many on the family property. As an African-American, his ancestors were slaves. Early generations of blacks in this area were owned by the Nathan Boone family. Father Berry's great-grandmother was Caroline. When she married William Berry after being freed, they started a forty-acre homestead. In 1873 William and Caroline built the house where the priest was born and now lives with his wife, Magdalena, and their two children, Dorothy and Elijah.

Father Berry left Ash Grove for many years. When he was young he wanted to leave the area and when he grew older he wanted nothing more than to return to the land of his youth. When he returned, he had goals to fulfill. He wanted to start an Eastern Orthodox Christian Church, which happened rather quickly.

He named the church *Theotokos*, which means "the one who gave birth to God, or God bearer," a reference to the Virgin Mary, the patron icon of the church. The full name of the church is *Theotokos Unexpected Joy Orthodox Christian Mission.*

He also opened the Ozarks African-American Museum, which displays artifacts from the rich history of his family and his race. The museum includes an old padlock from his great-grandfather Wallace White's slave chains. Wallace was the first black soldier in the Union's 6th Missouri Cavalry. Other items in the museum are a massive neck iron, leg shackles, trunks of old quilts (some dating from before the Civil War), a cabinet that was a present from Nathan Boone, and a medallion from A. G. Brock Slave Trading House, advertising "strong healthy slaves."

One might think that it would be hard for Father Berry to live in a community that includes the families of former slaveholders. But Father Berry takes a healthy approach to the history and often accepts speaking engagements to educate others. He is in much demand as a resource on local African-American history. He has served as a consultant on diversity issues at Missouri State University's School of Education. He is a featured speaker at the annual African-American and Ancient Christianity Conferences. He also travels all over the nation as a guest speaker and worship leader.

When Father Berry is not busy with speaking engagements, tending to his church flock or with the museum, he is working on his restoration project. His great-grandparents set aside a plot of ground as a cemetery for slaves, paupers, and American Indians. Father Berry is working to repair damage to the old tombstones and to restore the landscape to its former glory.

When he speaks to groups, Father Berry shows his ancestor's chains and tells them that "It is part of our collective history. You have to step back to look at history or it gets too emotional." He said. "I take advantage of everything around me to explain this or else they wore these things in vain."

Father Moses Berry was recently honored by the Missouri House of Representatives for all of his work and received a resolution from his state representative, Jim Viebrock.

Reverend Mary Ellen Waychoff, Macon County

Reverend Mary Ellen Waychoff doesn't have a church home—she has three. She leads services at three different churches every Sunday in Macon County. The churches are Ethel Presbyterian Church, United Church of New Cambria, and United Church of Bevier. She was the pastor of a small rural church in Oklahoma and was looking for a change when the chairperson of the Macon County Larger Parish pulpit nominating committee contacted her. When Reverend Waychoff heard that she would be pastoring three congregations, she was hesitant but went ahead with a phone interview. During this conversation, she felt that she was being called to take the position.

After the phone call she reasoned with herself about the challenges of the job, but she says that her own words kept coming to her as an argument as to why she should give it a try. Small churches need to share resources wherever possible, she always believed. After pastoring the three churches for more than five years she felt that it was a perfect fit that God ordained. Reverend Waychoff also makes hospital visits, helps with the New Cambria choir, plays the piano during services in Bevier, does much of the office work, leads Sunday night Bible study for all three churches and leads a youth group.

Virginia Huston, Pennytown

Virginia Huston is the keeper of this community that has been all but forgotten as time passed. The town, known as a black hamlet, was started with one man's dream to own land, as a freed slave, and to give others with a common past the opportunity to do the same. Joe Penny bought the first parcel of land in 1871 and continued to buy acres and divide them into plots, which he sold to other black settlers. By 1900 there was a total of sixty-four acres to Pennytown and forty families living in the community. A white landowner had allowed the residents of Pennytown to build a church on his property in 1886 and a few years later the trustees of the church bought it for $20. Eventually Pennytown built another church, school, store, and two community lodges among the small framed houses.

Virginia was the last person born in Pennytown, which now consists of a cemetery, the church, and one remaining frame house. Her interest in Pennytown was passed down from her mother who was given an assignment to write a paper about the community, after getting in trouble at school. Her curiosity was piqued as she visited with elderly people who filled in information about the roots of Pennytown. She spent much of her life doing genealogy of the founders and residents.

In 1988 Virginia's mother submitted a nomination for Freewill Baptist Church and it was added to the National Register of Historic Places. Her mother also raised money to repair the old church, having bake sales, selling quilts and compiling a Pennytown cookbook. The funds reached the amount of $18,000 and the restoration of the church was underway. The stained-glass window behind the pulpit displays a cross with broken chains reminding Pennytown descendents of what was overcome and that nothing is too heavy a burden.

On the first Sunday in August Pennytown descendents come from all over the nation to the small church. Everyone sits under the large shade trees to enjoy a potluck dinner. The highest attendance has been around three hundred. The church is not open but Virginia or one of the directors is always happy to give a tour and share the history of Pennytown.

Bishop Alonzo Monk Bryan and the Dude Ranch Drive-In Methodist Church, Maryville

Picture it: Maryville, summertime 1952. The church was the First United Methodist Church under the pastorate of Alonzo Monk Bryan. The summer was hot and Monk Bryan was having problems getting his congregation to patiently sit in the hot church for services. At this time air conditioning was not a part of everyday life. Monk Bryan remembered something that he had heard about a church in California, which held services outdoors. He talked to the owners of the local drive-in theatre and his congregation then made a revolutionary turn.

At age thirty-seven, Monk, as everyone called him, stood atop the Chuck House concession stand preaching in the glory of God's creation. The service started early, at 7:30 a.m., every Sunday from June through August. People liked the privacy of their own cars. At a time when people wore hats to church, there was no need to be so formal worshiping in the car.

Contrary to the indoor service, there was always a good crowd at the drive-in. At least fifty cars would stop at the entrance to pick up a one-page bulletin before claiming a spot on the grassy field.

The Chuck Wagon housed the piano and special music was always planned. From the drive-in's speakers that were hooked to the car windows, the preacher's voice reached each family. Ushers walked from car to car taking up the collection, which averaged a dollar per adult.

Monk's ministry in Maryville lasted eight years, but the drive-in church continued until 1976. Air conditioning was installed at the church in 1982. Monk would later become a bishop of the Methodist Church.

Jeanie Leeper, Versailles

Matthew 25 Ministries was born when home healthcare and hospice nurse Jeanie Leeper was burdened with the task of caring for people who she worked with that seemed to fall through the cracks of assistance and insurance in the Morgan County area. She would go to her pastor at the United Methodist Church she attends and ask if there was anything that the church could do to help. She was surprised one day when he said that perhaps there was something she could do.

Jeanie applied to work as a missionary for the Church and Community Ministries of the Church. She was accepted and quit her job to start the Matthew 25 Ministries concentrating on the message in verse 40 of that chapter where Jesus says, "I tell you the truth, whatever you did for one of the least of these brothers of mine, you did for me." Through the ministry and with the help of donations she is able to help many. Some are hardworking people who are stuck in situations they aren't able to change. The ministry helps in other ways too. Jeanie feels she is a true nurse to individuals now, not just treating the physical but being a friend and treating the mental, emotional, and spiritual health as well.

Reverend Eloise Marx, Scott City

Reverend Eloise Marx, a modern-day circuit-riding pastor, has served at two churches—Broadway United Methodist Church in Scott City and the St. Paul United Methodist Church in Commerce—at the same time. In her career, she has pastored many churches in this way. She originally started working with the Salvation Army and transferred her ordination to the United Methodist Church in 1954.

In the years from 1954 to 1970, she pastored five churches. In 1970 she decided to fulfill a longtime dream and get her education degree. She had attended seminary as a young adult, but this time seven of her twelve children joined her in college at Kirksville. Even though she began teaching eighth grade, she still stayed on the circuit and from 1974 to 1993 served in Bates, Macon, Lewis, Montgomery, and Scott Counties.

Richard Smith, Ralls County

Richard Smith often asked himself questions about how he got here and how things came to be the way they are. Richard is an African American from Ralls County near Vandalia. He wondered about how he came to be in Northeast Missouri and so started the long search of finding the answers. Salt licks, as it turns out, were the reason that his family came to the area. As slaves, they were moved to work the salt. Smith looked for older people to talk to in the area only to find that he was the oldest black man in the county. His mission is to research and do genealogy of the common folks, saying that famous African Americans have been researched but not just everyday people. Smith spends his time getting acquainted with his computer, not using one until he turned seventy, writing a book, *The Rough Side, How I Got Here*. He also speaks to local groups sharing his findings to educate others. He always begins by saying, "I'm not here to hurt feelings. I just want to tell ya what I found. You had nothing to do with this and neither did I." Richard Smith is pastor of Faith Tabernacle.

Father Tolton, Brush Creek

Augustus Tolton was born April 1, 1854, in the Ralls County community of Brush Creek, to Peter and Martha Tolton. The newborn child was regarded as the property of slave owner Steven Elliott. With the Civil War breaking out, Augustus' father reportedly fled to join the Union army, as did many others. Augustus' mother, meanwhile, was left to care for their three children. Fearing what might happen if she and her children remained in Missouri, Martha escaped from servitude taking the children by boat across the Mississippi River to Quincy, Illinois.

In the post–Civil War era, Father Tolton lived in a very trying time, due to racial prejudice. Father Tolton showed what kind of man he was, however, by continuing to push toward his goal despite barriers that often blocked his path. "What he was was a man who tried to rise above the times that he lived in. He was a person who was not prejudiced himself. His parish was as open to white people as it was to blacks. He could very well become a symbol of a life that can be led in the midst of very harsh prejudice," said Reverend Landry Genosky, a student of Tolton's life.

Shortly after coming to Quincy, Father Tolton attended the all-black Lincoln School and later enrolled at St. Boniface parochial school. However, prejudice forced him out of St. Boniface after one term, and he was subsequently admitted to St. Peter's school, headed by Father Peter McGirr, one of Quincy's first integrationists. Father McGirr was among the first to see the potential in young Tolton, who showed an early interest in religious matters and was a good student, graduating from St. Peters with distinction.

Augustus was taken under wing by a number of Quincy clergymen, who tutored him privately. In turn, Tolton worked with several local priests in providing for the spiritual needs of Quincy's black Catholics. His education received a major boost when he was permitted to enter St. Francis College, the forerunner of Quincy University. Tolton showed promise as a potential candidate for the priesthood, but efforts by local priests to place him in U.S. seminaries proved futile because of his race.

Finally, these efforts paid off when Tolton was admitted as a priest candidate at the College of Sacred Propaganda in Rome in March 1880. After six years of intensive study, Tolton was ordained on April 24, 1886.

The following day, he said Mass for the first time over the tomb of St. Peter in Rome. Father Tolton said his first Mass in Quincy on July 18, 1886, at St. Boniface. The following Sunday, July 25, he was installed as pastor of Quincy's St. Joseph Church, a black congregation.

Father Tolton became known for his excellent sermons and attracted many blacks and whites to his church. But after a while, many whites stopped coming because of the prejudicial sentiments aroused by Father Tolton's early success. These racial pressures escalated, making Father Tolton's stay in Quincy difficult. He finally asked to be removed, and was assigned to Chicago, where he organized a black parish called St. Monica's. He remained in Chicago until his death July 9, 1897.

From his humble beginnings in Brush Creek, Father Tolton became an inspiration to many. Despite leaving Missouri at an early age, he still has a strong following among those who believe faith should be open to all.

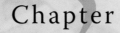

Chapter 5

THE WORKS THY HANDS HAVE MADE

The sun reflects on the water
Light sets and dances
The waves ease with motion
As night advances
The Son reflects on the soul
Love to all advances
Surrender comes softly
As communion dances
—LCK 2006

*M*issouri has a multitude of stunningly ornate churches and other man-made structures for worship; however, many people find that their best time communing with God is spent outdoors in the natural world.

There are vast caverns around the state that open into great rooms decorated with stalagmite and stalactite formations. Rivers and creeks transverse the landscape, and limestone bluffs reach toward the sky above. Wildlife great and small can be found living in lakes, prairies, and woods.

A ride on the Katy Trail, whether long or short, will transport you into nature and ease your mind so that you can be thankful for the beauty all around. The closeness of the Maker is all-encompassing when we take time to enjoy the gifts that He has given us.

Walk into the woods and observe the great intricacies of a tree—its root system, its bark, its outstretched branches, and its great veil of leaves, each with tiny veins and structural threads. Think about the care that God reveals in its creation. If He spent so much time and design on a tree, then what time, effort and care did He take when creating us?

Other blessings include outdoor chapels built to bring formal worship closer to nature. A few of these special places are featured in this chapter.

Shrine of Our Lady of Sorrows, Starkenburg

The Shrine of Our Lady of Sorrows is a place of great beauty and peace located in the rolling hills near Rhineland. Since its beginnings it has attracted pilgrims wanting to increase their faith. It includes the shrine, St. Martin's Church, the Grotto of Lourdes and Mount Olivet, Stations of the Cross and an underground sepulcher with a statue depicting Christ laid in the tomb.

The shrine grew out of St. Martin's parish, which began as a log structure in 1852. This church would become home to the *Weisse Dame*, German for "White Lady," a statue of the Virgin Mary. Whenever the parish conducted a procession the White Lady was carried in their midst.

When the stone church was built in 1872, a larger statue replaced the White Lady, which was stored in the attic. On October 27, 1887, Father George Hoehn, from Heppenheim, Germany, became Pastor of St. Martin's Church. Father Hoehn was a zealous, friendly man, and the simple piety of the people at his first mass with them impressed him. He was delighted that the natural surroundings of his parish so closely resembled his homeland. August Mitsch, Father Hoehn's nephew, came to St. Martin's on November 2, 1887, to serve as a sacristan.

In the year 1888, during the month of May, near St. Martin's Church a dogwood was in its full beauty, covered with hundreds of fragrant blossoms. In the attic of the monastery, which now served as the rectory, August Mitsch found the old, white, faded statue of the Blessed Mother. This he took and placed in the midst of the flowers of the bush. A more beautiful canopy for the Madonna could not have been imagined. The addition of a few candles completed the May altar. The place of devotion was soon discovered. August Mitsch, with the aid of two students, the Reverend Fathers George Koob and Jacob Denner, built a new log hut, to replace the one built in 1852, to protect the White Lady. It was so small that hardly two persons could kneel within, the rest had to kneel outside. The number of the faithful who frequented the woodland shrine increased rapidly, and the hut was soon replaced by a small chapel, octagonal in shape, which was also constructed of logs, with a small steeple to the front. Stained glass windows from Germany further enhanced it, and a bell was immediately hung in the tower.

The Stations of the Cross were erected in the Feast of the Seven Dolors, April 12, 1889. The first stations were very simple. In 1900, Joseph Highberger purchased new stations; pilgrims who visited donated the fourteen niches. After forty years, the stations were eroding and suffered damage from falling trees. In 1949, they were rebuilt of reinforced concrete.

The first pilgrimage made by people other than parishioners was on September 8, 1892, by the Catholics of Hermann. The tradition continues, along with many special events held throughout the year at the shrine. The semiannual pilgrimage at the shrine takes place in May. Pilgrims carry a replica of the White Lady in a rosary procession through the shrine grounds, with mass held at the outdoor altar. The daylong event includes a traditional German meal.

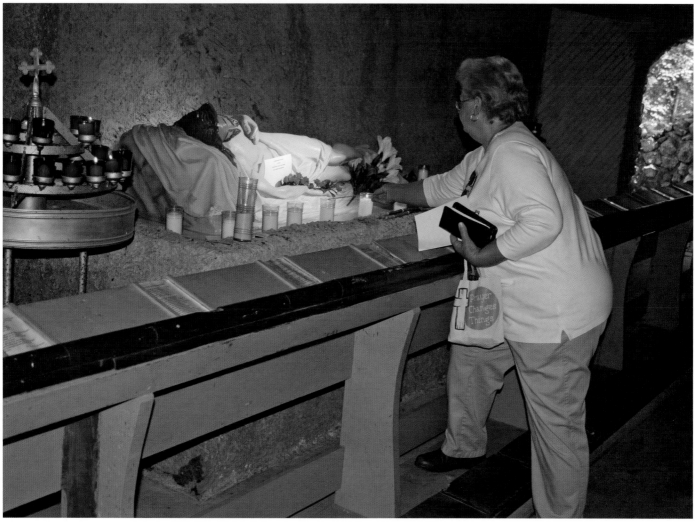

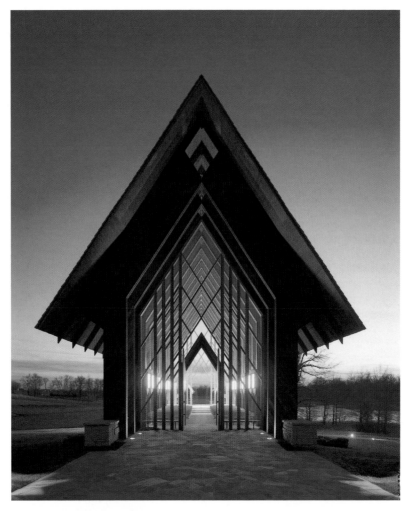

Marjorie Powell Allen Chapel, Kingsville

Although this nondenominational chapel is not exactly a natural formation, its walls of windows allow nature inside. The chapel is a treasured location for weddings and other appropriate events. Designed by architect Fay Jones, the cha-pel is located at Powell Gardens, a nonprofit organiza-tion near Kingsville. It is named for the older daughter of George E. Powell Sr., a prominent Kansas City businessman whose family is still involved with the organization's operations. Marjorie enjoyed the peacefulness of the park during her youth, and later provided funding for the chapel.

The chapel was designed to blend nature and architecture. The chapel's front glass wall sits closely to the lake, embracing the water's edge. A woodlands backdrop shelters the chapel entrance with a natural presence. Once inside the angular Gothic doorway, visitors marvel at the intricate patterns of wood that seem to make the light and shadows dance.

Powell Gardens describes a visit to the beautiful landscape as a "road trip for the soul." The gardens' history dates to 1948, when George Powell Sr. pur-chased the 915-acre tract. Besides the chapel, you can observe the Creator's works at the conservatory, an island garden, meadow, perennial garden, rock and waterfall garden, and through many changing events held on the grounds.

St. Jordan's United Church of Christ, Jeffriesburg

Many churches have outdoor places in which to worship, and St. Jordan's is one of these. Organized in 1856, this congregation first held services in a log weatherboard building. The original name was St. Jordan's Free and Independent Protestant Evangelical Church. In February 1892, the congregation decided to construct a new building that was dedicated on September 16, 1893. A parsonage and schoolhouse were added in 1896 and 1900, respectively. Stained-glass windows were installed in 1949.

On March 19, 1948, a devastating tornado damaged the church and many homes. Its destructive blow felled the steeple and caused the rear wall to cave in. While immediate repairs were made to the back wall, the tower was closed in without a steeple. It took forty-three years, but on Friday, July 19, 1991, a new steeple was set in place on top of the tower.

On December 30, 1950, the women of the congregation were granted the privilege to sign the church register and the right to vote. In 1957, pew communion was inaugurated and the name was changed to St. Jordan's United Church of Christ.

The outdoor Memorial Chapel was dedicated in 1981, and the first Easter Sunrise Service was held here. The outdoor chapel is used for services and is a special place for couples to get married.

Olivet Christian Church (Disciples of Christ), Columbia

Olivet Christian Church (Disciples of Christ) is another church that likes to worship outdoors. It is located four miles east of Columbia on State Route WW.

The original building was built in 1874 on land donated by Richard S. and Cordelia Estes. Members cut and hauled logs with teams for the church and that building still stands.

An educational wing was added in the 1950s, which later burned and was then rebuilt. In 1995 an entirely new church was built on adjacent land. The new church was designed to replicate features from the original building. Olivet Cemetery, established in 1874, is located between the two churches. A Bible Garden/Outdoor Worship Center was added to the grounds in 2005. Plans are underway to add a Christian Life Center with educational and recreational facilities.

The Olivet Church has a history of continuous growth with many young families participating. Since 1995, when the new church was occupied, the congregation has doubled. The full-time minister, who has been with the church over twenty-five years, and a youth and education minister, serve over four hundred members. Some members of the congregation have worshiped at Olivet for several generations. Parent-supported youth activities are a big part of the church program, including several annual mission trips.

On the third Saturday of June, Olivet holds its annual Mutton and Chicken BBQ serving between two thousand to twenty-five hundred dinners. In 2007 the church celebrated the fiftieth anniversary of the BBQ. Proceeds from the BBQ are divided between the church's building fund and outreach programs including the youth program, and local charities.

Mother's Wall, National Shrine of Mary, Mother of the Church, Laurie

Mothers are special people, so much so that since 1908 a day in May has been set aside in honor of all mothers. In Laurie, you will find the National Shrine of Mary, Mother of the Church, named for the world's most famous mother but devoted to all mothers.

The outdoor shrine is located on the grounds of St. Patrick's Church, which has been placed on the National Register of Historic Places. It occupies a natural grotto surrounded by trees.

A large revolving statue depicting Mary as a young mother dominates the site. The fourteen-foot-tall stainless steel sculpture has her arms outstretched, as if welcoming all to her embrace. It towers over the black granite Mother's Wall base on which sons and daughters have commemorated mothers living and deceased by paying to have their names inscribed in the stone.

From the base of the statue a waterfall and a fountain join the chorus of ever-present songbirds to make this a peaceful spot to relax.

This is a place to walk in solitude past the avenue of flags, to sniff the fragrance of twenty-five thousand flowers when they are in bloom or to take part in one of the weekend services while seated on the terraced hillside.

The shrine is located just north of Laurie on Highway 5. For more information call (573) 374-6279. A Web site can be found at www.mothersshrine.org.

Stonegate Glass Chapel, Walnut Shade

If you're looking for a beautiful setting for your wedding, the Stonegate Glass Chapel is a great place to have your big day. Located just ten miles outside of Branson, the Stonegate Glass Chapel is a nondenominational chapel with walls of glass to let in both the sunshine of the afternoon and the tranquil colors of evening.

You'll also get a beautiful view of Branson's rolling, forested hills from the walls of glass. Being an excellent setting for weddings, the chapel is furnished with accessories such as a Bose sound system, a baby grand piano, and a bride's dressing room.

You'll also find the Meadows of Eden reception hall conveniently next door to the chapel. The hall is elegantly decorated in a Southern style, which includes chandeliers and a grand staircase. Both the chapel and reception hall seat 150 guests.

Adam-ondi-Ahman, Daviess County

Adam-ondi-Ahman is a historic site along the east bluffs above the Grand River in Daviess County that according to Joseph Smith Jr., the founder of the Latter-day Saints movement, is the site to where Adam and Eve were banished after being cast out from the Garden of Eden and is to be a gathering spot prior to the Second Coming of Jesus Christ. On this site Smith discovered what he believed to be Adam's altar of sacrifice. During his time the area was also called Spring Hill.

Most of the site is now owned by the Church of Jesus Christ of Latter-day Saints and it remains predominately farmland. Many members of the church make pilgrimages to this and other historic Mormon sites in Missouri. Along with Heritage Plaza in Independence and nearby Far West south of Chillicothe, it is considered one of the "Crown Jewels of Church Identity."

The site is open to visitors, who can sit under shady trees on the hillside and look down into the long valley and read some of the history on bronze plaques. The constantly whispering wind speaks to guests here as a voice from the past, recalling the tragic events that took place here when the Mormons were driven from Missouri. It's a peaceful setting that is well maintained by the church.

The Black Madonna Shrine and Grottos, Eureka

Nestled in the beautiful foothills of the Ozarks west of St. Louis, the Black Madonna Shrine and Grottos offer a galaxy of dazzling mosaics and multicolored rock sculptures. Dedicated to the Queen of Peace and Mercy, the shrine is a shining example of what one man of faith can achieve. The grottos, which are constructed of Missouri tiff rock mined at Potosi, are set in a countryside atmosphere that refreshes the body and soul. The shrine and grottos are part of the five-hundred-acre Franciscan Mission.

The origins of this religious setting trace back to 1927. Among the Franciscan Missionary Brothers who that year emigrated from Poland to the St. Louis area was Brother Bronislaus Luszcz. He was a man driven by an overwhelming faith and love for Our Blessed Mother Mary.

In his native Poland, Mary is revered as the Queen of Peace and Mercy, and her most famous shrine is at the Jasna Gora (Bright Hill) monastery in the town of Czestochowa. The people lovingly refer to Mary as Our Lady of Czestochowa, the Black Madonna.

As a young man, Brother Bronislaus would sit by the road and watch pilgrims as they passed through his village on their way to Mary's shrine. Overcoming tremendous hardship, some of them walked for hundreds of miles, sleeping by the road, to reach their destination. The memory of these people — the difficulties they overcame and the love and devotion they had for Mary — remained with him throughout his life.

Brother Bronislaus wanted to share his faith with others by spreading the glory of Our Lady of Czestochowa. So, in 1937, he began his lifetime labor of love. Clearing the thickly wooded land, he built a beautiful cedar wood chapel and hung a portrait of Our Lady above the altar. The chapel soon became a center of religious devotion, with numerous pilgrimages, prayer services, and masses being offered.

Then, one Sunday evening in 1958, an arsonist started a fire on the altar. The brothers tried to douse the ensuing inferno, but flames consumed the chapel, leaving a pile of cinders. Today, however, the Black Madonna Shrine and Grottos continue to serve as an important site for the religious who visit.

Lady of St. Joseph Shrine and Schnurbusch Karst Window, Apple Creek

With so many caves and other karst features located in Perry County, it's not too surprising that at least one church would be built nearby such a feature. That's the case with St. Joseph Catholic Church at Apple Creek (formerly Schnurbusch).

An unusual "karst window" offers a window into the vast underground drainage system that underlies Perry County, which claims the most caves of any county in Missouri. In a sinkhole to the northwest of the church an underground stream comes into view as it emerges from a cave opening, plunges over a small waterfall, under an arched bridge before disappearing into a second "swallow hole" cavern.

Seeing this wonderful creation of the master, church leaders built a small outdoor altar and amphitheater in which services are held on occasion. The Lady of St. Joseph Shrine was completed in 1973. The entire area is tastefully landscaped, forming an appropriate place for meditation made all the better by the views and sounds of this natural wonder.

St. Jude's Chapel, Montauk State Park

St. Jude's Chapel is a traditional log cabin structure located just outside Montauk State Park. It is home to a number of local residents as well as a large number of fishermen and other outdoors lovers during the local trout fishing season, which is from the first of March to the end of November. It is set in a lovely pine forest with grounds conducive to real meditation.

Old Bethpage Church, Bethpage

"Where the Bible is the Standard" reads the sign on this Bible Baptist church. Bethpage is located in a quaint rural setting nearby a small spring whose running waters add greatly to the services.

The Irish Wilderness, Wilderness

In the mid-1800s a Catholic priest, Father John Hogan of St Louis, had a dream of a place where Irish immigrants could escape the oppression of urban life in St. Louis. With Irish men working on the railroads and women doing servant work for the wealthy in city homes, there was little opportunity for them to marry. The sense of community that had been their only happiness in Ireland disappeared.

In a wild area of the Missouri Ozarks Father Hogan, who was born in Limerick, Ireland, found affordable land and established a settlement that would forever after bear the name of its first European settlers, the Irish Wilderness.

The quiet solitariness of the place seemed to inspire devotion. "Nowhere could the human soul so profoundly worship as in the depth of that leafy forest, beneath the swaying branches of the lofty oaks and pines, where solitude and the heart of man united in praise and wonder of the Great Creator," the future bishop would write in his memoirs.

The timing of the ill-fated settlement however was not right, as the Civil War soon erupted. The Irish Wilderness was caught in the middle, becoming a "no man's land," and was raided by both Union and Confederate troops as well as bushwackers.

It is not certain what happened to Father Hogan's Irish immigrants, but after the war they were gone. The mystery of the Irish immigrants is part of the character of the land today. Nature has taken over man's feeble attempts to tame the wilderness. Because of the efforts of the Civilian Conservation Corps, the Forest Service, and the amazing healing ability of the land, the Irish Wilderness again has regained the same character that Father Hogan found.

In 1984 the U.S. Forest Service set aside sixteen thousand acres of land near Whites Creek as a wilderness area, one of eight such places in Missouri. Here you can get a good feel for what the area must have been like when the Irish came here. An eighteen-mile hiking trail cuts through the middle of the area. The trail snakes through tall stands of shortleaf pine. Sunlight struggles to reach the forest floor, held back by the broad leaves of oak and hickory trees. On the ground, fungi poke through damp earth, in places trampled by the footprints of white-tailed deer.

Chapter 6

Offerings

Lord, I feel your presence all around
Your beauty in nature, from sky to ground
Your Comforter when times are tough
What I do for You can't be enough
You gave Your life to purchase mine
I am a branch, You are The Vine
Take my life, live through me
Once was blind, but now I see
—LCK 2006

$\mathcal{M}$issouri Churches host many social activities to provide their members and the community with the opportunity to share fellowship. Such activities are key to the church's growth. Many are organized as alternative events to those offered by other groups. They strengthen the church as a whole and also give members the chance to participate in events that incorporate their faith in a family-friendly environment.

🕊 WEDDINGS 🕊

$\mathcal{W}$eddings are one of the most popular activities held at churches. These special events bring together generations who want to give the bride and groom a faith-based beginning as a couple. Missouri churches offer some beautiful settings for this wonderful ceremony of two people uniting as one.

St. Jordan's United Church of Christ, Jeffriesberg

This outdoor wedding was conducted in the outdoor Memorial Chapel that is part of St. Jordan's United Church of Christ in Jeffriesberg. Easter Sunrise services are held annually in this picturesque setting in the woods.

Mt. Pisgah General Baptist Church, Silva

Getting married in an authentic log cabin church is something few couples can relate to today. But members of Mt. Pisgah General Baptist Church in Silva can have this experience at the only log church building still in use in Wayne County. It was erected near Clubb in 1857 and organized by Elder W. L. Gower, pioneer General Baptist minister of Wayne County. It had sixteen members.

The logs were hewn by L. A. Roach, William Pinkney White, and Daniel Matthews. In 1884, the church was moved and re-erected at its present location on Highway 67 about two miles north of Silva.

The church has never been inactive, even during the Civil War. In 1972–73, an addition was built using matching logs secured by Brother Wayne Page, pastor at the time. A basement was dug for the new addition, resulting in three classrooms and a choir space in the main auditorium. A steeple with a bell from an old school was also added. A multipurpose building was erected in 1992 beside the church and another classroom has been added between the church and this building. Total membership is forty and this is a very active church at the present time.

St. Joseph's Catholic Church, Neier

Newly married Jesse and Sarah Wright posed for this picture on the steps of St. Joseph's Catholic Church, Neier. The well-landscaped grounds, with their many towering shade trees and the small lake behind the church form a beautiful backdrop for wedding photos often shot by one of the parishioners, photographer Karen Wright of Wright Photography in nearby Union.

 BAPTISM

*B*aptism is another part of Christian life. Some churches have inside fonts to welcome new members into the church. Others take to the traditional way of baptizing in rivers, creeks, and lakes.

Bethlehem Missionary Baptist Church, Halfway

In the summer of 1997 "Catfish" Lockhart, an older man at Halfway, told Donald Bybee (a Missionary Baptist preacher) that if he would hold a revival he wanted to come because he was lost. Donald was out praying for "Catfish" and looking around where he could build a brush arbor and have a revival.

The Lord told him to build it up at the site of an old falling down barn. He thought it was hopeless. He went home and told his wife, Reva, whose mom, Marie Ratcliff, gave her blessing. Marie donated the land for the church and cemetery. On September 1, 1997, the first revival was held and church services have been held there ever since.

The church has the old-fashioned altar with the cherubs protecting it. There's the star representing

God's spirit to lead us. The seven candlesticks represent the seven churches of Asia. The ladder represents Jacob's ladder, and the angels are going up and down the ladder. The candles on the ladder are for the ones who have been saved there and told about it. The tapestry behind the ladder was brought back from Iraq by Matthew Forrest.

There is a fountain representing God's living water, where you will never thirst again. There is a tomb, representing where they buried Jesus. Another well represents Jacob's well.

Believers Bible Chapel, Union

The following are pictures of members of the Believers Bible Chapel, two miles west of Union. The church does not have a baptistry, and new believers are usually baptized in the Bourbeuse River. When the Bourbeuse is at flood stage other measures must be taken. These two were baptized in swimming pools, one in the local YMCA and one at the home of a church member. Both of the children were baptized by their fathers.

First Baptist Church, Brookline

Lynn Swadley, pastor of First Baptist Church in Brookline in the 1950s, performed these baptisms in Terrell Creek between Republic and Clever. In 1862 the Union Baptist Church was organized in Little York, two miles southwest of the present village of Brookline. A frame house of worship, erected in 1872, was sold for debt to the carpenters, but was purchased and restored back to the church by Charles McClure. The present church was organized in 1882 on ground donated by the St. Louis–San Francisco Railroad. The church had a reported membership of thirty-five. The church and property was valued at $850. The community is rural, located twelve miles west of Springfield. The little village of Brookline is one mile south of the present church. Brookline was recently annexed into the city of Republic and much growth is expected for this area.

New Hope Methodist Church, Edwards

This baptism took place in the Osage Arm of Lake of the Ozarks. The church is New Hope Methodist Church that has been in existence in the town of Edwards since 1892.

Etterville Christian Church, Etterville

Originally known as Etterville Christian (Disciples) Church, this church organized on December 15, 1905. When the church reorganized in 1914, the name was changed. The current pastor is Borys Boyuk. Over the years, the church has participated in several activities. These include: Resurrection Sunrise Service and Breakfast, Revival Meetings, Vacation Bible School Retreat, Camp MoCoMi in Eugene, a church trip to Branson, Youth Nite program, youth group float in the Eldon Christmas Parade, Christmas dinner and program, and Christmas Eve Candlelight Communion service.

The church supports L.O.C.E.F. (Lake Ozark Christian Evangelistic Fellowship), M.O.V.E. (Missouri Operations for Vigorous Evangelism), and several missions. In 1947 baptisms were conducted in a nearby creek.

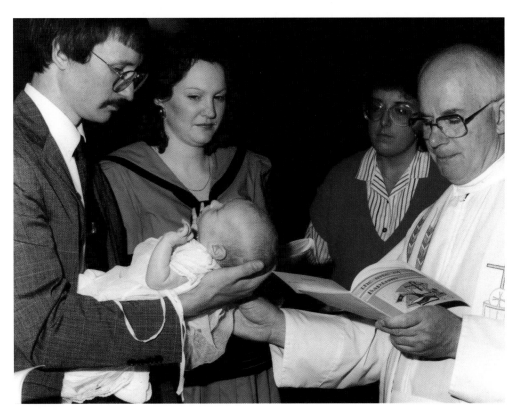

Immaculate Conception Church, Loose Creek

Father Michael Flanagan baptizes baby James McCarty in the name of the Father, the Son, and the Holy Spirit, using water from the baptismal font located inside the church. Catholic priests also make the sign of the cross on the baby's forehead with oil consecrated once a year at the Mass of the Chrism held in the diocese's cathedral and attended by all priests. Only the bishop may consecrate the chrism oil. The bishop is not able to baptize and confirm everyone in the parishes of the diocese, but his ministry is symbolically present in the chrism, which the priests and deacons will use.

*C*hurch picnics are always a lot of fun. In some parts of the state families never have to cook for themselves on weekends as the church picnics take place on virtually every weekend. When those are over the annual fall suppers take their place.

Olivet Christian Church, Columbia

In 1957 the Olivet Church BBQ began as a church fundraiser. In the beginning the men of the Church bought and butchered adult sheep for the mutton. Today just the best cuts are purchased and a long process is completed to get it just right for the BBQ.

The BBQ is a community event. The men begin cooking the mutton (leg of lamb) around 4:30 in the morning. Chicken cookers begin around 11:00 a.m. The green beans and potatoes are cooked in a large iron kettle outside. Pies are cut and then put on plates. Many of the pies are homemade and brought in by the members of the church. Tea and coffee are made, tables and chairs put up under the tent, and in 2007 the famous Olivet homemade coleslaw was brought back for the fiftieth anniversary celebration.

Neighbors and friends from the community and Columbia come to eat and socialize. The event provides an opportunity for the kids to get to know and work with the older folks of the church and also to see the community join the church in making it all happen. Over the years, it helped to develop relationships that still exist today on a personal basis and for the church.

The church has for many years shared proceeds from the BBQ with a variety of organizations in Columbia such as Habitat for Humanity, Eldercare, Cedar Creek Therapeutic Riding Center, and Granny's House.

*T*here are many forms of worship that are unique to individual churches and faiths. Church traditions help to involve as many people in the services and help to tie new generations to the faith of those who founded the church.

St. Francis Xavier Catholic Church, Taos

One tradition of this central Missouri church is the Living Stations of the Cross conducted by members of the church school's eighth-grade class during Lent, the forty days preceding Easter. Class members confiscate every bathrobe in town, construct cardboard swords for Roman soldiers, and vie for the honor of portraying Christ on his way to be crucified.

Another unusual form of worship is the pet service held on the feast day of St. Francis of Assisi. Children attending the school are invited to bring their pets, or something representing their pet such a as a dish or leash, to the afternoon service held in the garden behind the rectory.

Historic St. Patrick Church, Laurie

Four priests co-celebrate mass at historic St. Patrick Church, a beautiful stone church in Laurie. This church was founded in 1868 by Irish immigrants and is the oldest church in Morgan County. It was placed on the national register of historic places in 1979. These co-celebrated masses are held on special occasions at Catholic churches in Missouri.

Gentry Christian Church, Gentry
Sometimes turning off the lights adds greatly to services. A couple at Gentry Christian Church reflects in the moment of a Christmas Candlelight service.

 # BRUSH ARBOR REVIVALS

*B*rush Arbor revivals were an annual event for many churches, especially in the summer and fall. These were temporary outside churches formed when the men of the congregation would take their axes and cut cedar poles and boughs to form a canopy that provided a little shade for the meeting. Rough-hewn logs often served as seats. After sunset, the stars, the moon, and the gentle hiss of Coleman lanterns provided the light. Many a sinner found religion at these revivals.

Bethel Presbyterian Church, Bay
Built in 1848, this church is made of native limestone quarried near Bay. The tower and steeple were added in 1889 and reach seventy-five feet. One tradition of this church was the Mission Fest, held annually under the brush arbor for two days. In the 1970s, the Brush Arbor was cancelled and services moved inside. Bethel held an evening Christmas program with a twelve-foot Christmas tree. As late as the 1930s, a church caretaker would stand near the tree with a long pole with a wet cloth on one end to snuff out the candles when they became too short to be safe. Twenty-five pastors have served Bethel in its 158-year history. In 1993, Bethel was added to the Presbyterian Historical Society. The membership of Bethel Presbyterian Church decreased over the years, and the last regular service was held on December 25, 2005. The church is now used a few times a year, and its upkeep is through Salem Presbyterian near Hope.

Pine Ridge Church, Chadwick

In the 1960s Pine Ridge Church held a revival that is still talked about today. In July of 1965, Alva Walker was preaching a revival when the snakes first appeared. People came from all around as the story circulated. There were more than one hundred copperheads killed during the snake hunts that followed. Nestled in the beautiful Mark Twain National Forest between Chadwick and Forsyth, it was built more than one hundred years ago and at one time served as the Chadwick school. When the school moved, the building was sold for $1 to the Walker family who still maintains it today. As late as the 1950s, coal oil lanterns provided the light and a pot-bellied wood stove the heat. Although the lanterns and wood stove have been replaced by electricity and gas, the outhouses are still in use.

IN SERVICE TO THE LORD

A labor of love is how the thousands of people who volunteer to care for Missouri's churches would describe their work. Many are the stories of how members of the congregation gave from their hearts with both money and sweat to build, remodel, maintain, and grow their churches.

Bethel United Methodist Church, Cainsville

In 1856, this church began by meeting in homes. Services were moved to Cavanaugh School in 1868 where they remained until the building was destroyed by a storm. While clearing the storm debris, the church's Bible—dry and undamaged—was discovered beneath the overturned pulpit. The old pulpit and three benches (used for pews in the first church building) salvaged from the storm are now cherished pieces and are still used occasionally. The current building was built in 1894.

Several changes have been made to the building since that time, many of which were funded completely by the women. The women of the church replaced the building's foundation in the 1940s, and they also sanded the sanctuary's thirty-five-by-forty-foot wood floor and the twenty-by-twenty-four-foot kitchen floor, finishing both with layers of varnish. These determined women also painted the exterior of the church while wearing dresses and aprons. Some even wore heals as they stood on ladders to paint.

Palmer Church, Palmer

When thieves broke into the Palmer Church they burned down the historic one-hundred-year-old structure to cover their tracks. But those who held the church near and dear to their hearts decided to rebuild it. Donating the money needed, they rebuilt it exactly like it was before, inside and out, and in the same location. The old church was a school, place of worship, and a place to call home. Its remote location has a spring, where someone wrote on the stone "When you drink hear think God." There's also a grave for an unknown soldier who died during the Civil War. The site is located fifteen miles southwest of Potosi. The town was named for the Palmer Lead Company.

Immanuel Lutheran Church, Pilot Knob

Immanuel Lutheran Church began when August Gockel came to Pilot Knob in 1858 to work as a carpenter/cabinetmaker for the Pilot Knob Mining Company and could not attend a local Lutheran church. His former pastor helped him

start a Lutheran church that was attended by both Lutherans and Catholics (there was no full-time priest in the area until 1870). In 1861, the Lutherans drew up a constitution, named their church "German Lutheran Evangelical Church of the Unaltered Augsburg Confession" and built their new church building. In 1874, the church joined the Lutheran Church Missouri Synod. Gockel helped build the exterior of the building, but the one-piece altar-pulpit reflects his purest inspiration and symbolizes the doctrine of Law and Gospel. On the alter stand a French-Catholic crucifix and two candlesticks that were gifts to Gockel and his wife from her family. The inscriptions over the entrance are the name and date of the church and a German translation for Romans 1:17, "He who is righteous through faith shall live." The three-thousand-pound bell bears the inscription, in German, "Come, for all things are now ready."

With the Civil War and the approach of the Battle of Pilot Knob to secure control of Fort Davidson in 1864, the little church was tagged to be a field hospital and command post for the Union Army. A large bloodstain on the floor of the parsonage room in the back of the church attests to its hospital status.

Immanuel Lutheran Church remains the example of a typical small-town 1860s church. Changes have been slight. The original glass, kerosene chandeliers have been made electric and the wood stove, though still in place, has been replaced with a furnace. The two back rooms and schoolroom are now a museum where pastoral robes worn in the 1860s, Civil War artifacts, and other memorabilia can be viewed.

The Lyceum Theatre, Arrow Rock

The Lyceum Theatre now resides in the 1872 Baptist Church in Arrow Rock. Founded in 1961, it is the oldest professional regional theatre in Missouri. The church now serves as the lobby; the two-row slave balcony of the church is still intact. This structure was used in a 1972 movie about Tom Sawyer that was filmed in Arrow Rock.

Lighthouse Christian Center, Dexter

Pastors Tim and Tina Russell began this ministry in 1993 when God inspired Pastor Tim through a vision.

The ministry sits on forty-three acres of ground, where Crowley's Ridge, the only hills in the otherwise flat Bootheel of southeast Missouri, crosses Highway 60. The lighthouse structure, an old grain silo, supports a War World II relic that lights the sky for miles as it sweeps the horizon with a symbolic message that Jesus Christ is the light of the world.

Shrine of St. Patrick, St. Patrick

When the Reverend Bernard Patrick McMenomy changed the name of St. Marysville, Missouri, to St. Patrick he made this town the most Irish of any spot in Missouri. People come from all over the state on St. Patrick's Day to get cards stamped in the only St. Patrick in the world with a post office. While there they never fail to tour the Shrine of St. Patrick, which was built by the Reverend Francis O'Duignan thanks to donations from people of Irish ancestry. The shrine was fashioned after St. Patrick's memorial Church of the Four Masters in Donegal, Ireland. It is Celtic in design with semi-circular, recessed doorways, a central rose window, gable Celtic crosses, and a belfry with a circular stairway leading to the choir loft. The circular bell tower is highly unusual. Inside the shrine are thirty-six stained glass windows patterned after the *Book of Kells*. Besides the St. Patrick's Day festivities, the area comes to life again when the church hosts its Fourth of July picnic.

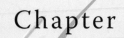

Chapter

7

A JOYFUL SOUND

Walnut tree
Stands tall and wide
Life flows through veins
Safe inside
Bark covered
Trunk and branches
Budded limbs
Color enhances
Leaves constructed
All the same design
The whole created
The Maker shines
—LCK 2006

$\mathcal{G}$rowing up as the daughter of a preacher and being in church whenever the doors were open, I looked forward to the music that always accompanied the service. Many of the choruses and hymns I heard had been written over the years. Many have rang through the churches for more than a century. Some churches I attended had only a piano for accompaniment; others brought additional instruments into the mix.

There was Prospect Baptist Church in Bois D'Arc, where a gentleman played the mandolin and the banjo; there were larger churches in Springfield that included an organ. As I grew into my teens, there were churches that used drums, tambourines, and guitars for more informal worship. By the time I was a young adult, I attended High Street Baptist in Springfield and Calvary Baptist in Republic and these churches had an orchestra as part of their music ministry.

Along with the stringed, woodwind, percussion, and brass instruments the voices of the congregation added other harmonies. Soloists, duets, trios, quartets, and small groups along with choirs, sing the songs of faith in their many parts to bring a rich full sound to Christ's feet as a way of worship and praise. I will never forget being at High Street Baptist Church when the congregation sang "Wonderful Grace of Jesus" with all the parts. It was like being a member of a two-thousand-voice choir!

Following are some interesting facts about how churches use music in their worship.

Coldwater Church, Wright County

In 2006 the Coldwater Church in Wright County held its Decoration Day, marking the one-hundredth anniversary for this event. The celebration included music, speeches, and dinner. Decoration services at the church first began in 1906. Paper flowers were made for the graves and the tradition of music and plays began. It was the time of year when families donned their new "decoration" attire. Everyone brought a dish for dinner on the grounds. The tradition continued over the years, being held on the fourth Sunday in May. Graves of loved ones are still decorated in the cemetery, which has 294 graves. The oldest marked grave is for Elizabeth and Jasper Neil, who died in 1870, twenty-two years before the existing church was built. There are eleven Civil War veterans, one from World War I, nine World War II veterans, and one from the Vietnam War in the cemetery. Music plays a big role in the annual celebration.

Immanuel Lutheran Church, Pilot Knob

Historical Immanuel Lutheran Church in Pilot Knob remains very much like it did in 1861. The original reed organ is in the sacristy. This historic church still has many of the original fixtures and furniture: the pulpit, altar, pews, chandeliers, wall sconces, eighteenth-century French altar crucifix, candle set, and silver communion set. The school has the original desks, blackboards, and books.

St. Paul's Episcopal Church, Ironton

A few members of St. Paul's Episcopal Church in Ironton gather around the piano singing hymns. St. Paul was organized in 1869 and has had services continuously since then. Judge Emerson donated the land and the building plans, and the community, including nonmembers, participated in constructing the present building through donations of materials and labor. The building was finished in 1870 and the first service was held on Christmas Eve of that year. The building remains very much in its original form, although it has modern lighting, heating, and air conditioning. Its style is called "wood gothic." Its roof is steeply sloped, with cypress shingles, which are painted in a diagonal pattern. Its windows are period stained glass. Its original walnut pews seat about 105 persons.

Quimby Pipe Organs, Warrensburg

Organs contribute greatly to the praise and worship that takes place in Missouri churches. But keeping these massive and complicated instruments in working order is a monumental task. Fortunately, Missouri is blessed with a business devoted to organs, Quimby Pipe Organs in Warrensburg.

When Michael Quimby was only nine years old he took a tour of the First Methodist Church in Stillwater, Oklahoma. It was love at first site. His interest grew as he grew. He started researching and reading anything he could get about the way pipe organs work and are designed. In 1970 Quimby Pipe Organs became a reality.

This business belongs to the Associated Pipe Organ Builders, Inc. There are only twenty-six companies in this elite group, and membership is by invitation only. Quimby Pipe Organs has a strong reputation for the work and creativity they put into an organ. They were asked to restore the organ in the largest Gothic cathedral in the world, the Cathedral Church of St. John the Divine in New York City.

The company also has a reputation for the sound of its organs. Eric Johnson, the head "voicer" is responsible for the sound, which he says is both technical and emotional. Depending on his mood, a sound might differ slightly from day to day. The metal or wood is then manipulated to have the appropriate sound and resonance. Michael Quimby is proud of his staff's self-motivation and dedication, one of the reasons that operating Quimby Pipe Organs rates closer to pleasure than work.

Prince of Peace Cathedral, Highlandville

So much about the Prince of Peace Cathedral speaks of the past. This small cathedral, the smallest in the world according to the *Guinness Book of World Records*, was once a simple stone washhouse. This building is more than one hundred years old with an exterior of native Ozarks stone. Today it is a chapel of peace and quiet reflection for its tiny flock of followers of the Christ Catholic Church, a denomination of conservative Catholics that split with the Vatican a century ago over church doctrine. Archbishop of the Christ Catholic Church Karl Prüter bought the seventeen-acre piece of land in 1983, longing for a place where he could write religious books.

It wasn't long before Prüter was inspired to turn the washhouse into a cathedral. Pews were added as well as kneeling rails, altar, a fiberglass one-thousand-pound onion dome, and a stained-glass window depicting *Christ as the Prince of Peace*. The most recent addition was a gift to the church and to the Lord that was given by parishioner Mark Chartier. He constructed a tiny pipe organ to fit in the fourteen-by-seventeen-foot space. It was made of forty-two wooden pipes, the lowest being made at a ninety-degree angle because there was not enough height in the cabinet to accommodate the three-foot pipe. Bamboo pins hold it together.

The instrument is constructed much like the fourteenth- and fifteenth-century European pipe organs. The maker speaks of the humility required to play the organ with a sensitive touch and an appreciation for simplicity. The organ was dedicated in 1998.

The cathedral and organ may be seen daily as masses are held in the tiny cathedral, which seats fifteen.

Bethany United Church of Christ, Berger

The congregation of Bethany United Church of Christ near Berger has never been a wealthy one. But when the elders made plans to build their new church in 1869, they spared no expense to ensure a lasting place in which to worship, opting to use stone in its construction.

Later they would add a Kilgen pipe organ that today is a rare find in a country church. The organ was installed in 1904. It originally stood in the curved balcony, but in 1929 was moved to the front of the church, where it is located today, because for a while the pastor was the only one who could play it.

"The people, they were very poor," recalls Harold Schutt, who serves as the church's caretaker. "Grandma supposedly gave $7 toward the purchase of that organ."

To keep costs down members of the congregation made the pews from walnut lumber cut from area farms. However, no expense was spared on the huge bell that was added to the church in 1887. The purpose of the bell was to help the pastor communicate with the far-flung congregation in the days before telephones.

Reverend J. J. Holtz was the pastor of the church when the bell was installed. His name was cast into the side of the bell in appreciation of his twenty years of service to the church, making him the longest reigning of the church's forty pastors. Holtz was so proud of the bell that he rang it three times a day every day of the week. Ringing the bell is still an important tradition at the church. It's rung at 8 a.m. to announce the death of a church member. It also tolls at sundown on Saturday night to herald the coming Sabbath.

Schutt, who replaced his uncle as the Bethany bell ringer, says he rings the bell when the sun is still "a fence rail high. That's when it's quiet. People listen for it. Sometimes they ask, 'Did you ring that bell?'"

He says the one-thousand-pound bell will lift a full-grown man off the floor if he's not careful.

Gentry Christian Church, Gentry

Carolers from the Gentry Christian Church go out every year spreading the Christmas cheer to all in this part of northwest Missouri. The Gentry Christian Church was first organized at a meeting held on January 30, 1910. The church was known at that time as the Church of Christ of Gentry. A short time later the present church building was erected on land donated for a church site. On June 12, 1966, a fiftieth anniversary service was held at the church on Sunday afternoon for the purpose of rededicating the church to the glory of God, the teaching of the Gospel and salvation, and to help spread the growth of the Kingdom of God upon the earth. In 1993, the church body voted to become a nondenominational church but to retain the name Gentry Christian Church.

Handel's *Messiah*, Columbia

Jane Smith had always listened to recordings of George Frideric Handel's *Messiah* during the holidays, but had never seen the oratorio live until Columbia's Christmas Chorale performed it at Jesse Hall at the University of Missouri campus on December 7, 2006.

The chaplain at Fulton State Hospital said she was captivated not only with the music, but with watching the gifted musicians manipulate their instruments to play the complicated movements.

"The *Messiah* is a great way to do Christmas that doesn't involve tinsel," Smith said following the 2006 performance. "I've always been touched by the biblically based words, but I couldn't believe the performers' giftedness. I especially liked when the music would just involve the sounds of the single base, the single cello, and the single violin."

Chorale artistic director Alex Innecco said the brilliance of the *Messiah* is how dramatic, yet accessible the music is for audiences. Brazilian-born Innecco has changed each year's performance slightly since the group began performing the movements with the Columbia Civic Orchestra in 2002.

"The *Messiah* is three hours long, and as beautiful as it is in its entirety, we are competing with TV and busy schedules, so we pick and choose parts of it to create about a one hour and forty minute performance," Innecco said.

The Chorale also hosted a *Messiah* sing-along at the Missouri United Methodist Church. Solos were sold on eBay to raise money for the group's mission to promote high-quality choral music in the community.

Tenor Paul Peterman, who has sung with the Chorale since August 2006, said audience participation in the sing-along developed a deeper appreciation for *Messiah*.

"The sing-along was such a holistic experience," said the environmental chemist for the U.S. Geological Survey. "When we perform, I usually get a sense that people are enjoying the music. But when audience members joined in the chorus parts, I felt like the meaning of the music was coming to life."

Columbia Handbell Ensemble

The delicate chimes of a handbell choir sound like poetry in motion, and have long been a crowd favorite during the holiday season. One of the longest running community handbell groups, the Columbia Handbell Ensemble has held holiday concerts throughout Missouri since 1988.

"Bells are so versatile," said Edward Rollins, cofounder of the group and associate pastor at Columbia's First Baptist Church. "Some bell arrangements are quiet, deeply spiritual and thought-provoking, yet others just make your toe tap and make you feel good inside."

Rollins said he has enjoyed his more than twenty-year involvement with church bell choirs. He says the religious focus of song choice often excludes contemporary favorites like, "Up on the Housetop." The community group transitions from classical carols, such as "Carol of the Wise Men" to off-beat jingles like, "Shiny Stockings."

The ensemble of about thirteen volunteer ringers from mid-Missouri travels the region to play for schools, civic clubs, and churches during the holiday season.

The Plattdütscher Vereen von Cole Camp
(The Low German Club of Cole Camp)

This club was formed in January 1990 by a small group of people who were deeply involved in the planning of Cole Camp's 1989 Sesquicentennial celebration. As a result of this event, there was a renewed interest in the town's Low German heritage. Toward that goal, the group holds monthly meetings for people who want to continue the tradition of speaking this language that comes from the northern German regions. The entertainment usually includes some Low German skits, songs, and discussion of the history and heritage of Lower Saxony.

The group sponsors three music groups: the *Männerchor* (men's choir), the *Damenchor* (ladies' choir), and the *Kinderchor* (children's choir), which are active throughout the year. One highlight of the group's work is the annual evening of German Christmas music performed in one of the local churches in the Low German tongue.

Photo by Jenny Fillmer

Big Smith at Lonestar Church

Big Smith is a Springfield-based band that is difficult to categorize. The group's fans might be old hippies in tie-dyed shirts, twenty-something girls, rednecks in seed caps, and college professors still attired in their three-piece suits. The group plays everything from hillbilly-bluegrass jams to covers of rock music legends.

The group's second release was a live gospel CD that pays tribute to their family's musical roots. Recorded on an idyllic day at the one-room Lonestar church house in the Ozark hills, "Live at Lonestar" is graced by the singing of the extended family members in attendance, the same folks who passed down their musical heritage to the men of Big Smith.

The album, performed by the band along with many of their kinfolk, has all the appeal of an old-fashioned revival. Old standards on the album include "There's a Higher Power," "Streams of Mercy," "The River of Jordan," "I am the Door," "Old Time Religion," and of course, "I'll Fly Away."

Music runs deep in this family combo that includes descendents of some of Taney and Christian Counties' original settlers. "If you dig down deep in our family history you will find ballad singers," says front man Mark Bilyeu, who still plays his Uncle Chester's Martin D-18 guitar. "It died out but we revived it in our family. Grandpa Cupp was a ballad singer. I interviewed Grandma and she sang four of his songs for me."

Before her death in March 2002, Mark's Grandma Thelma often joined Big Smith on stage wearing red high-topped sneakers. The Lonestar collection features her singing a solo on "Land on That Shore."

"Grandma was a tremendous influence on our family," Mark says. "She was the first one to get saved. Her influence spread religion throughout our extended family."

Golden Road, Doniphan

There's nothing like Southern gospel quartet harmony to move an audience spiritually and emotionally. In 2004, an estimated twenty-five hundred people filled the Bess Activity Center at Three Rivers Community College in Poplar Bluff to attend Ozark Border Electric Cooperative's annual meeting. During the meeting Golden Road, a Southern gospel quartet based in Doniphan, sang four-part harmony.

"Midway in their song selection they sang 'I Pledge My Allegiance to the Grand Old Flag,'" says Joyce Boatner of Wappapello who attended the event. "They had only sang a couple of lines when everybody got on their feet and started singing. It was really a chilling experience to watch this."

Thousands of people inside dozens of churches throughout southeast Missouri have been lifted up by the harmony of Golden Road.

Brothers Dwayne and David Watkins, both of Doniphan, lead the group. Dwayne sings lead while David sings bass. Jerry Chewning sings tenor and Tim Tesreau baritone. Tim, along with David, has been with the group since its beginning. All four sing lead at times.

Jerry's the newest (but not the youngest) member, joining after Matt O'Neal left the foursome to pursue a music ministry degree.

The group's success has been impressive. Golden Road sang at fifty churches in 2001 and by 2003 that number increased to seventy-three. By the next year they reached out to eighty-two churches in Missouri, Arkansas, Mississippi, Kentucky, and Tennessee. They also attended three county fairs, five homecomings and other events, mostly within a two-hundred-mile radius of Doniphan.

The foursome crisscrosses the area on weekends in a gold Chevy minivan. Golden Road performs for donations at churches of any denomination.

"Whenever God puts joy in your heart you have to let it out. We want people to picture heaven, a place we're all looking forward to," says David.

Tim adds, "Some of our songs you wouldn't think would move a leaf across the road," he says. "But God speaks to different people in different ways."

Chapter 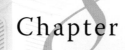 8

ALL ARE WELCOME

A church with steeple tall and steep
And true to its standards has this church been
Since its erection first began
Catering not to social rank, with love its only test
This church has sought throughout the years to all its best
It has given love to all of those who have bowed their heads in prayer
And comforted many a breaking heart
Who has sought for solace there.

—Glada Shultz

One common denominator with virtually all of Missouri's churches is the welcome you will receive when you stop by. Whether you are a newcomer to a small town or rural area, a tourist camping out in a state park, or someone in need of a church to call your home, you can find a place of worship in Missouri that will be happy to have you attend.

Oakland Christian Church (Disciples of Christ), Columbia

Oakland Church continues to occupy the original building, which was constructed in 1872. When first built at a cost of $2,400, it was a typical church structure measuring forty-two feet by fifty-two feet. Surrounded by acres of large oak trees, naming was easy for the forty-three charter members and their families. Tradition tells us that two doors were put into the front of the church building so that one could be exclusively used by men and one exclusively used by women. These two doors remained until the 1950s even though the practice did not.

New members were continually added and by 1910, there had been 157 members added to the original group. Revivals were held over the years to draw new members who were often baptized in neighboring ponds. Currently there are 124 members, some who are eighth-generation members. Attendance has varied over of the years with a slump during the early 1920s, an increase in the mid-1930s, followed by another slump during World War II. Although Sunday school was held generally every week, church services were held weekly, biweekly, or monthly depending on the numbers, and the church has never closed its doors. Special services have continually been held at Christmas and Easter, often presented by the children of the church.

In 1909, the Women's Missionary Society was organized, contributing to foreign missions as well as to their own church. This group evolved into the Christian Women's Board of Missions, then into the Women's Council, and is currently the Christian Women's Fellowship (CWF).

In 1952 an annex was added to the original structure, which provided room for community meetings as well as a much-needed kitchen. Five years later the education wing was completed, providing space for nine classrooms. In 1993, the last addition was completed of two additional classrooms.

Over the years, Oakland has developed a strong tradition of social events. Mutton and ground hog suppers have been replaced with hog roasts, turkey dinners, and ice cream socials. The pancake breakfast and the mother/daughter banquet occur annually as well as the traditional Christmas and Easter celebrations.

One memory of the church comes from Jay Turner, whose family has been active in the church for generations. When church members expressed an interest in adding a steeple to the roof, Jay's dad woke up in the middle of the night following a dream on how to build the steeple.

In the winter of 1957 he built the steeple in his shop. Many of the men from Oakland came to his assistance. He needed a weatherproof covering that would look good for many years to come. So he bought aluminum sheeting and fashioned an old crosscut saw with a smooth back side to make a brake that would put a series of bends in the metal that would lock each panel together the way siding works today.

It was built on a heavy wagon made to haul logs to the sawmill. When it was finished the wagon hauled it to church on a Saturday morning and a crane was there to lift it to the roof. The roof had been modified with large treated timbers to bolt the thirty-five-foot steeple in place. A bell house was added around the connection of the roof and the steeple and a bell was added.

When it was finished the Turner family could see the cross on its top for many years until tall trees finally blocked it from sight.

Old Peace Chapel, Defiance

In 1799, Daniel Boone led his family from Kentucky to the picturesque Femme Osage Valley located near Defiance. There, Daniel and his son Nathan built a four-story, Georgian-style limestone home modeled after Daniel's boyhood home in Pennsylvania.

Nathan sold the home in 1837 and several families lived there over the years. In 1998, the Andrae family, who owned the property at that time, donated it to Lindenwood University.

Since then, the university has expanded beyond the home tour by adding Boonesfield Village to its preservation efforts. The quaint village situated behind the Boone home allows visitors to catch a glimpse into early nineteenth-century life on the Missouri frontier. The settlement is comprised of more than a dozen historic buildings, with more to be added. Visitors will see a log schoolhouse, a log general store, a log barn, a gristmill, and a milliner's shop on the tour.

One highlight of the village is Old Peace Chapel, which is a charming relic of local Americana. The original structure was built between 1838 and 1860 just five miles from the Boone home.

Moved to the village in 1983, it has been restored to pristine condition. Sixty percent of the glass is original. The other 40 percent was made in Germany using nineteenth-century techniques. A working pipe organ and church bell add to the chapel's charm and the numerous weddings that are held there each year.

Between 1860 and 1898, the chapel was used for a number of purposes. It was a church, meeting hall, and a merchant's store. In 1898 a group of people organized a congregation and held regular services in the chapel. Six years later, the Evangelical and Reform Church recognized the group as an official part of its congregation.

The steeple was added to the façade in 1904. Legend has it that the congregation knowingly made it higher than the steeple on the nearby Lutheran church. The clock, made in St. Louis by Philip Pohland in 1865, is designed to ring three bells—two on the quarter hour and the third on the hour.

The Old Peace Chapel is now nondenominational. It can seat one hundred people.

The Daniel Boone Home and Boonesfield Village are open daily from 9 a.m. to 6 p.m. For prices and information, call (636) 798-2005 or log onto www.lindenwood.edu/boone.

Holy Family Catholic Church, Freeburg

Drivers passing through Freeburg on Highway 63 often pull over to marvel at the sight of Holy Family Catholic Church, dubbed the "Cathedral of the Ozarks" for its incredible grandeur.

The church was established in 1904 and a temporary wooden church was built in 1907. It was a thirty-by-fifty-foot structure with a sixteen-foot sanctuary and a fifty-foot bell tower. The parish pastor was Reverend Gerard Fick, who had a dream of building a more impressive brick church for the town.

The process began with the quarrying of local limestone for the foundation in 1920. During that same year a cornerstone was laid and the names of local people who contributed to the church building, coins from the time, pictures of the old church, and periodicals from 1910 to 1920 were placed in the cornerstone as a time capsule.

By 1921 the new church was dedicated. It was designed in the Romanesque style, and is 127 feet long by 45 feet wide. It took 513,000 bricks to build.

Today there are 252 families who are active in the church. Each year since its establishment there has been a parish picnic that is held on the Sunday of Labor Day weekend. More than fifteen hundred people are served at the dinner.

The people of Holy Family welcome visitors to this historic church.

Shiloh Tabernacle, Quincy

The Shiloh Tabernacle is an open-air structure that has housed generations of religious services with a history dating back 150 years. It is typical of the early structures that went a step beyond the brush arbors that were used for revivals and were more temporary in nature.

Logs for the tabernacle came from trees at the location. Hand-hewn beams held together by wooden pegs supported the roof. Benches made from long wooden planks provided seating.

The church history book notes that before the tabernacle was built a brush arbor had been erected, but it was burned by bushwackers during the Civil War.

Years ago, families came to this spot for weeklong religious meetings. Sometimes they lasted longer than a week, depending on the preacher. The faithful would camp out on the site, returning home to do chores and when they were finished, returning for more preaching. Some brought their milk cows along.

Those attending came on log wagons or walked, often putting on their shoes only upon arriving at the site. Early revivals often generated a great deal of noise as repenters saw the light and joyously vowed to change their ways.

Afterward, those attending would sit in the shade of the tabernacle and visit, while feasting on refreshments brought from home.

Over the years the structure fell into disrepair. Finally Gary Myers, the former pastor of Shiloh United Methodist Church, got the ball rolling on rebuilding it before it was too late or someone got hurt.

The new pastor, Reverend Phillip Fennell, continued the efforts, getting permission from the church to carry out the remodeling, provided all the materials and labor were donated. A special account was even set up at United Missouri Bank in Warsaw where donations could be made. Other churches contributed to the restoration project.

Efforts to repair the historic structure with so many memories continue, with repairs being made in much the same manner as they were when it was first built.

Those working on the restoration hope to see it used again for reunions, weddings, Bible camps, funerals, and as a wonderful place for all to worship God in open-air revivals.

St. Louis of France Catholic Church, Bonnots Mill

St. Louis of France Catholic Church is located at the top of Church Hill Street overlooking the French town of Bonnots Mill. Members celebrated the one hundredth anniversary of its founding in August 2005.

The white frame building was built in 1905 on property purchased by Archbishop John Glennon from Edward and Mary Favier. Purchase price for the property was $6.

Each year on the second Sunday in October church members play host to the annual Fall Festival. People from all around the area come to enjoy the home-cooked country ham and sausage dinners with all the trimmings. Games, a country store, raffle, live music, and other attractions are also featured.

Approximately eighty families from in and around Bonnots Mill call St. Louis Church their place of worship.

Rutledge Baptist Church, Rutledge

This northeast Missouri church was organized August 31, 1889. The present building was erected in 1894. It was dedicated on the fifth Sunday in August of 1897. It has one of the tallest steeples of any other Baptist church in the association. Its doors and windows are unique and it is well maintained. The poem on page 136 sums up the feelings of one member of the congregation, Glada Shultz.

Galena Community Church, Galena

At the Galena Community Church, the lighted belfry and steeple cross are a welcome sign for all. The church has been giving Christian care in southwest Missouri for more than 120 years. It is the oldest active church in Stone County.

It began from Sunday schools established in Stone County by Tom and Sallie Porter in 1883 and organized as a Methodist Episcopal Church in 1887. Stone County had religious Sunday school trailblazers such as James McCullah, Bud Scott, and Kate G. Yocum whose schools helped to form the church.

People today sit in twenty original pews, which were shipped from Germany during 1888, the same year the church was built. Today the church has no official association with any other churches or organizations.

Galena Community Church literature speaks of being "generous to Christians." The church "walks the talk" when it comes to being an independent, interdenominational church. The church acknowledges that there are many Christian beliefs and many forms of baptism.

In these matters, Galena Community Church accepts the Christian's choice. They accept all Christians to serve in capacities of ministry and leadership regardless of race, color, or gender. The church has an "Open Table of the Lord" and all believers in Jesus Christ are welcome to receive communion.

The church is host to the 9/11 Day of Prayer. The music of the church is a blend of traditional and contemporary.

In 2004, the historic church was crowned with its first steeple. The product of many helping hands, it was placed on the rooftop on a Saturday, requiring most of the day.

Typical Sunday attendance is 73, with a membership of 69 persons eighteen and older and a record attendance of 122 set in December 2005, breaking the former record of 108 set in December 2004, which broke a seventy-year-old record of 103 in 1928. A number of members of the congregation are also members of other churches. Some of the financial support comes from individuals in Missouri, Arkansas, Oklahoma, and Texas. New financial records have been set each year since 2003 and a number of improvements have been made possible by this generosity.

Members of the church say, "If you do not have a church home and are looking for a place to worship in an atmosphere of acceptance, then GCC is the place to be! We're glad to include you in our Christian fellowship."

143

Bethel United Methodist Church, Wildwood

In 1858, a group of Southern Methodist preachers were holding a camp meeting near a spring at a place called Camp Hollow in west St. Louis County. It was at this particular 1858 camp meeting that Bethel United Methodist Church credits its start. A year later, a stone church called Rock Bethel was dedicated on Wild Horse Creek.

Bethel, which means "House of God" in Hebrew, survived the bitterness of the Civil War, although membership was untrusting between the Unionist Germans of the region and the members and especially the preachers of the then-Southern Methodist Church.

The pastors covered circuits, which changed from time to time, but the church survived. After the Civil War, the church was moved from the rock church into a log building in Gaehle's Grove, at the junction of Wild Horse Creek and Hardt Roads. There are two traditional stories told to give the reason for this move: one that the church had outgrown the rock building; and a second that the church never held and could not get ownership of the land on which it was built.

Bethel had twenty-nine members in 1873, so there is some doubt the first tradition is correct. The log church supposedly was built for the Sunday school and a temporary place for preaching until a better church could be built. It never was formally dedicated.

By 1872, the membership announced it was looking for a suitable site for a new building. In March 1873, the St. Louis Marble Company donated two acres on Manchester Road. Additional land was purchased from that company for a cemetery.

The new church was dedicated in April 1875. People came, some by horse-drawn buggies and wagons, others on foot. The congregation was never large, especially by modern west St. Louis County standards. However, the warmth of Christian friendship and commitment kept Bethel what it was meant to be, "God's House."

By 1924, the kerosene lamps were replaced with electric lights, the church had a new roof, and "the Aid" (the Ladies Aid) embarked upon one of the lasting traditions of Bethel Church, the Chicken Supper. The first was a cold supper, with each of the ladies preparing a large picnic basket and bringing it to church. By the second year, a Manchester tinner had made a vat for deep-frying and Bethel's Chicken Dinner had become an annual event that reaches far across the community. A good meal was and continues to be sold to raise money for Bethel's annual (United Methodist) Conference contribution.

With the westward population movement filling many of the far corners of St. Louis County and beyond, Bethel's membership continues to grow. Current membership is nearly 250 families. Still, the early rural beginnings and attitudes of Bethel United Methodist Church carry forward in many ways. Visitors and new members constantly comment about the warmth and friendliness, the genuine reflection of God's Love, which is so much a part of its congregation.

Forsyth United Methodist Church, Forsyth

The Forsyth United Methodist Church began as a dream of a small Bible study group in 1978. The dream became a reality in 1979 with the church being chartered with forty-eight members. There was no stopping these people of spirit who made the financial contributions for the church building, its altar furnishings, railing and light fixtures. On July 1, 1980, only one year from chartering, two hundred people gathered for the Service of Consecration.

They didn't stop here. In 1982, they added Sunday school rooms, a Fellowship Hall and kitchen. The year 1987 brought the purchase of the parsonage and an organ. Enter the twenty-first century and continued dreams brought into reality a much larger sanctuary, more Sunday school rooms, a sound and choir room, a library, more offices, meeting areas, a larger nursery, a foyer with comfortable seating, and a Family Life Center with showers and a new larger improved kitchen off of it.

A large memorial stained-glass window looks over a garden meditation area and there are memorial stained-glass windows in the doors going into the sanctuary. The dreams and improvements have continued with a new and larger nursery and extended Sunday school area.

Many Habitat for Humanity groups actually live at the church while working on homes and the Family Life Center has been opened for use to many community functions as part of the Community Out-Reach program. A Cub Scout troop, working with a local camp for troubled girls, a Mission group that gets out their hammers and nails building homes in Mexico, a nondenominational support group for people who have lost loved ones are just a sample of the Out-Reach program which continually grows.

As the church grows, so grows the spiritual life of this flock living the church's mission statement: To be Christ-like individually and as a body; going beyond our walls offering Christ to others.

The Episcopal Church of the Transfiguration, Mountain Grove

The first service of this mission church was held June 17, 1890, as organized by James Archer. At the time it was named St. Mark's. Services were held in a room above the drugstore owned by H. E. Stiff, a member of the congregation. Later the services were moved to another location.

In 1935 it was decided to buy a lot and build a church. On Whitsunday, 1935, the Reverend Roy Fairchild held a field mass on the farm of Louis Rathbone Bever just east of Dunn, Missouri, and a dedication to start the new church building. More than two hundred Episcopalians from seven counties attended.

Mr. Bever designed the building and supervised its construction. Lester Dickey, a local stonemason, used native fieldstone for the exterior. Church members did most of the interior work in the church.

Bishop Robert Nelson consecrated the building on December 10, 1935, and the name was changed to the Church of the Transfiguration. Other churches donated the altar, altar cross, communion rails, and other furnishings, which date from 1901 to 1908. Six hanging lights, which were made by Todd and Les Lower in 1936, are still operating. The church bell, which was donated by Mrs. Paul Shepard in 1935, is still rung for services.

The first priest to serve St. Mark's was Reverend M. M. Moore in 1890. Since 1890 there have been thirty-two priests and deacons who have conducted services and more than seventy lay readers.

In 2003 a new parish hall, designed by congregation member William Marx, was dedicated and named in honor of Reverend Fairchild. He and Robert Hart, also a member, supervised the construction and outfitting of the hall. The congregation is active in community service.

Members come from Cabool, Norwood, Ava, Houston, Hartville, Graff, Willow Springs, Bucyrus, Huggins, and Mountain Grove.

Macedonia Cemetery working   August
New church house   4th Saturday

Built in 1906 and all finished
by 4th Saturday in Aug. at which
time the building of the church
was celebrated and cemetery
cleaned

Macedonia Methodist Church, Grandin

This church sits on a hillside some twelve to fifteen miles north of Doniphan and a few miles south of Grandin where the Missouri Lumber and Mining Company was headquartered from 1888 to 1912.

Now owned by the Ripley County Macedonia Cemetery Association, it hosts the Homecoming on the fourth Saturday in August. This event turned one hundred years old in 2007.

The exterior of the church is much as it was when completed and is a monument to simpler days. It is still furnished very much the same as when it was built.

A historic photo has this caption written on it: "Macedonia Cemetery working new church house. Built in 1906 and all finished by 4th Saturday in August at which time the building of the church was celebrated and cemetery cleaned."

St. Paul's United Church of Christ, Cooper Hill

St. Paul's, Cooper Hill, was one of several congregations in the area started by a minister from the Evangelical Mission Society of Germany, Reverend August Rauchenbusch. Reverend Rauchenbusch went from one area to another meeting in homes.

Timothy Leach, a member of the Cooper Hill group, donated land for the church and also for a public school. The church was organized and a building built in 1882. The church was called "St. Paul's Evangelisch Kirche."

In later years the Evangelical Church and the German and Swiss Reformed Church merged and became the Evangelican and Reformed Church. Later the E&R Church merged with the Congregational Christian Church and became the United Church of Christ, known as the U.C.C. Church.

Hampton Presbyterian Church, Everton

"I do not know if there was a church organization at the time or not, but a revival was held in August of each year in a the one-room school. One year the school was locked when people arrived for church. Jimmie McGehee had been hired to hold the meeting, and finding the schoolhouse locked, he said maybe the devil was locked inside and sent the men home for their axes and they built a brush arbor across the road from the school," recounts Mrs. Belle Hastings Bowman. She was a charter member of Hampton Church and attended Hampton School.

On April 27, 1881, four acres of land was deeded to the Pleasant Ridge Cumberland Presbyterian Church. The church burned in the early 1930s and a new church was built. On March 1, 1914, the church was reorganized as the Pleasant Ridge Presbyterian Church of U.S.A, and soon after (because the church was so close to the older school) was referred to as Hampton Church.

In 1981, it was the centennial year for a nearby town, Everton. Many activities were held throughout the year. On one Wednesday evening there was a brush arbor meeting with all the area churches joining together for the special evening.

La Due Christian Church, La Due

La Due Christian Church is located in Henry County. Henry County records show that people have been buried in the cemetery since the 1850s. The earliest records indicate that the town owes its existence to the MKT Railroad with the earliest census reported in 1870. The church is still active and burials have taken place in the cemetery as recently as 2005. Few residents remain in La Due, a town that once held a population of over three hundred people. At one time, the town had a bank, three churches, an elementary school, post office, grain elevator, two groceries, and was on the main line of the MKT Railroad. It's a much different place than the Ladue that is an affluent suburb of St. Louis.

Brushyknob Freewill Baptist Church

Brushyknob Freewill Baptist Church was established on November 9, 1929, with twenty-five charter members. The church is nestled in the Ozark hills of Douglas County.

Its name came about because of the landscape of the area. The church is located in a brushy area on the knob of a hill. The name not only stood for the church but for the entire community. At the time it was formed, this was the only church in the area. It began as a one-room building with a wood stove. After years passed classrooms and a small basement were added. The building also served as a community building. Church was held at this building every year until August 2005, when a growing congregation decided it needed a bigger building. The new building is located three miles from the original.

Antioch Christian Church, Everton

The first entry in the old book records the organization of the "Church of Christ at Antioch Meeting House, Dade County, Meeting" as being effected "on the second Lord's Day in May 1844."

The first house, built in 1845, was made with logs with a mammoth fireplace on one side. The second house was built in 1898, and a third was built in 1905.

During the early days of the church, the people came by horseback or on foot. Later the first automobiles of the century made their way along the dirt roads in all kinds of weather. Dinner on the grounds was a common occurrence at Antioch, as this was the favorite socialization of this era and the women strived to show off their cooking. This still holds true today as Antioch continues to have dinner on the grounds each fourth Sunday after services.

Maple Grove, Reorganized Church of Jesus Christ of Latter-Day Saints, Stewartsville

Maple Grove was organized with six members on April 25, 1877. The members met in the White Dove Schoolhouse until they built the building now known as Maple Grove. Twenty members built the building. John Daries donated the half-acre for the church and gave $150 in cash and Henry Hinderks donated one-half acre across the road to be used as a cemetery. The construction of the building began in the spring of 1881 and finished that fall. Services are still held every Sunday.

Goodwill Chapel United Methodist Church, Sedalia

On any given Sunday, three miles southeast of Sedalia, one can hear the original steeple bell being manually rung at the Goodwill Chapel United Methodist Church as it has been done for the past 160 years.

The church arose from a brush arbor meeting in 1897 led by two evangelists, Reverend Mrs. Ella Thorpe and Reverend Mrs. Mattie Allison. The revival took place in a field approximately seventy-five yards west of where the church now stands. Enthusiasm and well-attended meetings brought thirteen charter members to organize and begin church on November 7, 1898.

On November 29, 1996, some church members received a call from local authorities reporting that pranksters had set fire to Goodwill Chapel. Members sprung from their beds and headed to the burning church. Quick action from a family nearby the church saved the structure. They heard the boom and saw the fire then called the fire department and the building was spared. After calling the authorities, the family went to the church with their own fire extinguishers to help put out the fire. Another Baptist church in northern Pettis County was also set on fire that same night, but that building didn't have the same good fortune as Goodwill Chapel. Their church burned to the ground. Donations received for the repair of Goodwill Chapel were gladly given to the congregation of that less fortunate church.

Salem Lutheran Church, Farrar

The Salem congregation was formed on May 16, 1859. Those members weren't part of the original East Perry County Saxon settlement, but were some of the Saxons who moved to the area in the 1850s. These folks established the Salem Lutheran Church because they were tired of commuting the far distance to neighboring churches.

The church building was built in 1866. Each side of the building has arched two-story windows with the interior having a wrap-around balcony, pulpit above the altar, and an arched print stamped ceiling. The current pipe organ was dedicated on July 2, 1939. Since then the building has been remodeled in 1952–53 and 1985.

Today the congregation has about 370 baptized members. Church services are held every Sunday and all special church festivals. Not only does the church hold services, but also has a Christian day school that has had class since 1867.

Liberty Christian Church, Liberty

The first group of disciples met at the Clay County Courthouse and organized the Liberty Christian Church on April 9, 1837, with thirty-eight members. Those members first met in an old stone house, but in 1839 they built the first of three church buildings.

During the Civil War, Liberty was under the command of federal troops. The town was under order not to hold any public meetings. The chief elder at the time, Dr. William A. Morton, refused to obey these orders, and held church on Sunday. A soldier was sent to deliver a message to Dr. Morton saying that no church service was to be held. Morton replied, "I thank you sir, but I have orders from a higher officer than yours to have services and we plan to obey his command." Liberty Christian Church was the only church in the area to hold worship services.

When the second church building was erected the men of the church decided that a bell for the church would be an unnecessary expense. The women raised the money for the bell, and even collected jewelry to purchase silver for the bell. This building was damaged by a fire and was torn down. While building the third, now present, building the men saw no need for a church bell, and placed it on the curb to be hauled away. The women of the congregation refused again. A bell tower was built and that bell is still there today, ringing every Sunday.

Today the church is known throughout the area by its stained-glass windows. Those three windows were obtained when a church in Cincinnati changed hands leaving the windows without a buyer.

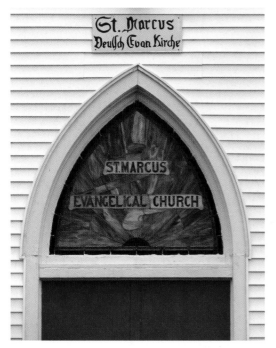

St. Marcus German Evangelical Church, Near Hermann

Church members are hard-pressed to tell visitors what town St. Marcus is near. That's because it is in the middle of nowhere. This church is at the intersection of Missouri Highway 94 and County Road EE, northwest of Hermann. The pure-white color of the church is nicely set off by a bright red welcoming door. German writing on the sign above the door signifies the ancestry of this beautiful rural *kirche*.

Saint Patrick's Catholic Church, Spring Fork

Saint Patrick's Catholic Church is located in Pettis County on "U" Highway in rural Spring Fork, Missouri. It is one of several St. Patrick's, the patron saint of Ireland. It is a lovely brick building with several interesting lightning rods on the roof. The church has quite a bit of fancy brickwork near the entrance. The old hand-operated water pump is still on the property.

United Methodist Church, Bellflower

The United Methodist Church of Bellflower is located on the corner of Montgomery and Broadway Streets. When the cornerstone was laid in 1905 this was a Methodist Episcopal Church. The town was then known as New Bellflower. A homecoming with special services to observe the fiftieth anniversary was held September 4, 1955. The celebration for the centennial anniversary was held on September 18, 2005.

Big Niangua Missionary Baptist Church, Roach

Big Niangua Missionary Baptist Church (also known as Roach) is located approximately six miles west of Camdenton on Highway AA in Roach, Missouri. This church house was built in 1951.

Recently, the church has had the electric wires replaced, new plug-in outlets added, and two new window air-conditioning units installed. With the ceiling fans and the air conditioning running, it stays pretty cool in the summertime. For heat, a traditional wood stove is used and church members just bring in firewood when needed. Outhouses, a throwback to earlier, simpler times, are still being used on the premises. There are also two cemeteries that are directly across the road.

There are revivals held at Roach at various dates and members there also attend revivals held by their sister churches (churches of the same faith). One revival in particular that gets everyone excited is the "Brush Arbor." Every year the second Saturday in July kicks off the revival. It's held outdoors underneath the "old brush arbor" approximately four miles past Ha Ha Tonka State Park in Camdenton. Every evening for around two weeks, people from surrounding towns come around and have worship services together. Guitars, fiddles, banjos, violins, and piano keyboard are some of the instruments used to make the music. Bring your lawn chairs or sit underneath the "old arbor."

Another event sometimes participated in is the fifth Sunday services. When there are five Sundays in one month, a sister church hosts a dinner and afternoon service. Usually several churches get together for a potluck-style luncheon and then have singing and another church service afterwards. Locations for these services are rotated among the churches.

When a saved individual wishes to join the church and become a member, they must give a testimony of their salvation and must be baptized. If they haven't been baptized before, they pick a date (so family and friends can attend) and the baptism takes place at one of the surrounding rivers. Even if it's in the middle of winter, we'll go down to the river. By doing the Lord's will, never has anyone gotten sick by this.

Big Niangua Missionary Baptist Church has services every Sunday with adult and child Sunday school at 10 a.m., regular services at 11 a.m. and evening services at 7 p.m.

The Union Church, Cole Camp

This historic old church was the first formed to serve the growing Anglo-American population in the area. The land was purchased from Ezekiel Williams in 1842 and a log church was erected and a cemetery established. The present church building was erected in 1904. The cemetery is large and historic with many well-known early residents buried there. The church and cemetery are located approximately two miles west of Cole Camp on F Highway.

Zion United Methodist Church, Indian Grove

Zion United Methodist Church is located at the intersection of Highways M and Y, three miles west of Indian Grove. The church was established in 1881 and since has celebrated two centennials.

Between the years 1875 and 1900, there was a large movement of families to Chariton County. The church building started out as a public schoolhouse, when two men began a "singing school." One of the young men brought a preacher who talked the group into organizing a Sunday school. The Sunday school grew rapidly and soon plans were made to build a church.

Visitors are always welcome, and all are met with warm greetings, handshakes, and hugs.

Immanuel Lutheran Church, Brauersville

The congregation of Immanuel Lutheran Church, Brauersville, Missouri, was founded in 1849. The first church was erected in 1859. The present church was erected in 1881 and is located on AD Highway just northeast of Cole Camp, Missouri, in Benton County. It is affiliated with the ELCA.

St. John's Catholic Church, Leopold

St. John's Catholic Church was built in the year of 1899. Work was begun in the spring. The church was built in pure Gothic style from native limestone found around and near the town. Parishioners of St. John's did most of the work on the church themselves. The church has undergone many interior changes.

In the fall of 2003, Bishop John Leibrecht announced that St. Anthony's Parish at Glennon would be a mission parish of St. John's. Formerly, St. Anthony's was a mission of St. Joseph's in Advance. This seemed like a good decision because many of the people in Leopold have relatives in Glennon. Also, the Glennon youth attend school with the Leopold students.

In May 1944, the Shrine of Our Lady Queen of Peace was dedicated to the members of the parish who were serving in the armed forces. Children of the community were asked to find the stones used to construct the shrine. After the shrine was built, evening rosaries were said for those serving in the armed forces. The prayers for the safe return of the servicemen have worked, for not one member of the armed forces that live in the Leopold parish have failed to return home alive.

The following is a poem called "The Bells of Leopold." It was written in 1931 by the late Vest Myers, former dean of Southeast Missouri State University.

The Bells of Leopold
At dawn across the eastern hills
I used to hear the clear-toned bells,
Now low and sweet, now loud and bold,
The ringing bells of Leopold.

I've heard then in the gay springtime
Ring out the merry wedding chimes,
In silver notes and not too bold,
Those gala bells of Leopold.

And sometimes on an autumn day
They say they sing a roundelay,
In softened tones—in notes of gold,
The mellow bells of Leopold.

I've heard that at the midnight hour,
Sometimes there creeps out from the tower
A solemn song, as days of old
Speak through the bells of Leopold.

And one day when a dirge was played,
And sadness hearsed both man and maid,
I heard them moan across the wold,
Those solemn bells of Leopold.

I've gone afar from childhood scenes,
But still there come to me in dreams,
Those memories sweet of joys old,
And I hear the bells of Leopold.

Little Oaks Chapel, Chillicothe

Little Oaks Chapel was built in 2004 in memory of Vern Wascher's mother, Anita, and loved ones the Wascher family has lost over the years. It is open year round with a guest book registry inside to welcome visitors. There are six pews in this tiny chapel. The stained-glass windows came from a church in England. There is also a beautiful stained-glass cross built by Vern and stained-glass work by Beardens Glass of Kansas City. It is located on the garden grounds in Livingston County at 4435 Livingston County Road 514.

Owasco Baptist Church, Green City

The Owasco Baptist Church was organized as a mission church by fourteen members of the Milan Baptist Church. There was no church building at that time so services were held at the local rural schoolhouse, in fields, and in homes. Usually the preacher was J. C. Pollard, pastor of the Milan Baptist Church. Owasco is located in Sullivan County, in Union Township.

The church was growing, so in October 1895, the church members purchased an acre of land from Arthur and Susan Brock, owners of the local general store. At this time Owasco was a thriving rural community with a store, blacksmith shop, and mill.

Plans to build a church were put into motion. Subscriptions from the local residents were collected. Many were monetary, but some were for labor and/or materials. The church was completed and dedicated on June 7, 1896.

The church measures thirty feet by forty feet. Originally there was a bell tower, which had to be removed because of structural problems. It was never replaced. The church still has the original handcrafted pews and pulpit, wood stove, and old upright piano.

This church was the religious center of the community as well as the social hub. Many activities were held here over the years, ranging from performances of the local ladies, Extension club meetings, 4-H club activities, political rallies, traveling theatrical performances, as well as weddings and funerals. Carry-in basket dinners on Sundays and holidays were frequent, and softball games following church in the field just to the south were a highlight. Everyone attended.

Then in the 1960s as families moved away, the church was closed and soon began to deteriorate as windows were broken, the roof began to leak and wild animals, mice, and bees took up residence.

In 1976, Joann (Cleeton) Tharp and her husband, Murlan, decided to restore the church. Joann, her parents, and grandparents were all raised in the community and her great-grandfather helped build the church. In fact, it was built on land that was originally owned by her great-great-great-grandfather, James Cleeton, who also established the cemetery just west of the church in the 1860s, so she had a special bond with the church.

With the help of family, friends, and many more wonderful people, the church was repaired and still stands today on top of a hill surrounded by farmland. It is still maintained today by Joann and her son, Craig. They host carry-in dinners on Memorial Day as well as other functions. The church was the site of a wedding in 1997.

A centennial celebration was held in May 1996 with 140 people in attendance. It is too bad the walls of these old churches cannot speak to tell about all the preaching services, revivals, Sunday School classes, Vacation Bible Schools, Children's Day programs, the singing and praising God, funerals, and weddings held here. Oh, what a message that would be.

Dardenne Presbyterian Church, Dardenne Prairie

This is a pioneer church established by a missionary pastor that counted some of Daniel Boone's survey party among its founding members. It was built on the site of the historic Naylor's Store on the Boone's Lick Trail.

Dardenne Presbyterian Church continues a remarkable history on the region and, yes, on the world too. Worship was first held in a store and then a log church. In the early days, congregates arrived on horseback, wagon, and an occasional carriage. On Communion Sundays, they brought basket dinners and stayed through the day until evening services were held.

In 1862, the brick church on Dardenne Creek was mysteriously burned to the ground two days after Union soldiers had attended services. Worship continued under a protective arbor on Dardenne Creek until 1868 when the Rock Church was built on the present site.

The first of the church's three cemeteries is maintained on that site today. Travelers or movers who died on the Boone's Lick Trail are buried in the "strangers" section of the cemetery.

Much of the present Dardenne Presbyterian Church was built since 1970 by the hands of faithful members—including the organ, which has thirty-six hundred pipes. The Adam Lamb Preschool is named after the Scott professor and member who taught area children from 1844 to 1878. Today's fifteen-hundred-member congregation thrives on worship, education, music, and local and international missions.

Full Gospel Union Church, Edgar Springs

This church was built in 1911 as the Bassinger Memorial Union Church. The people who donated the money to build this church also donated money to build a church at Lenox, Missouri, at the same time.

This was the only church in the community of Edgar Springs for close to thirty years. Different groups of church people would share the building each Sunday. They all had their own time to worship.

All area funerals were held in this building for many years. In the 1950s, Brother Woodruff set the church in order. He repaired the building and bought new seats. The church is now occupied by a Full Gospel group of people with pastor Fred Hamilton.

The church does still do water baptism at the river, usually underneath Yancy Mills Bridge. There is also an annual mother-daughter banquet, annual Christmas dinner with a humorous skit and an Easter dinner and egg hunt for the kids. They also host a Vacation Bible School each summer.

163

FULL GOSPEL
268 ELM
SUNDAY
0945 AM-0600 PM

Cedar Hill Baptist Church, Edgar Springs

This church is located two miles east of Edgar Springs on Highway H. It is one of the few remaining log churches in Missouri. The little church in the cedar grove is also the subject of some controversy concerning the date of its founding. One area history book mentions the date as 1860–1865. But Alvin Brookshire, grandson of the church's founder, says the church was built sometime during 1889. Charles Widener also said the later date was true, as he remembered the building of the church.

Whatever the date, the church came into being because William Fore, one of the four brothers who settled in the hills nearby, had a dream. Every night for a week, he dreamed that a particular crooked sapling stood on a nearby slope. Finally, he went to the spot, found the sapling, and decided to build a church on the spot.

Bill named the church and hung a sign above the door. The area had been cleared of timber so he planted two-foot tall cedars in rows around the church and up the slope. Soon afterward, the Reverend "Patty" Patterson started holding meetings in the church and they continued once a month until the 1920s. The church was put into trust, with a new generation taking over as the old one passes on.

Revivalists often use the church, probably because of its old-time quaintness and charm and the ease of filling its thirteen pews. Reverend Wilson was very strong on revivals in the church fifty years ago.

The cemetery on the slope above the church is the resting place of Bill Fore's son, Chris. Periodically from that time other graves have been added beneath the cedars.

Cedar Hill Baptist Church has withstood a lot in the last one hundred years. Several of the original cedars were burned or cut down, although some have been replaced by nature. The pulpit, stone, and some of the pews have been stolen and new windowpanes always seem to get broken. The chinking between the logs has been replaced many times. Money for the care of the church comes in small drops and trickles, and one can only guess whether Cedar Hill will stand another hundred years. It is used for the occasional wedding today.

Deerlick Baptist Church, Waynesville

Members consider themselves truly blessed to have this beautiful church to worship in. It was established on July 18, 1993.

Everyone worked together getting stuff done. Men from the Baptist Association in Eldon, Missouri, came and worked on the basement. Harry and Martha Snelling made the trip to Henderson, Texas, to get the steeple.

Today fish fries, Easter Sunrise Services, Christmas programs and monthly singings from April to November are held at the church. People come from neighboring churches to take part, bringing their singing voices and musical instruments.

The church features its own Kookie Kitchen Band, which performs at local nursing homes with their home-made instruments.

Peace Lutheran Church, Elk Prairie

This is a modest and humble church that has withstood more than one hundred years of change. The original 122-year-old structure still stands, and services are still being held there.

The church was founded in 1884 by German immigrant Johann Frederich Haas. The records of this rural church date from the 1880s to the present. Prior to 1924, they were written in German. Services at the church were conducted in German until 1939.

A few historic moments at Peace Church:

The first person confirmed was Clementine Adam on April 16, 1893, by Reverend George Mueller. The first baby baptized was Heinreich J. Kroiting on February 7, 1886, by Reverend A. W. Meyer of Rader, Missouri. The first couple joined in marriage was George Sachs and Karoline Adam on October 23, 1889.

The large pine tree in front of church was planted by Reverend Ed Schildt between 1925 and 1929. In 1928 the pastor was paid $360. That amount was raised to $450 in 1933. In 1941 new hymnbooks could be purchased for 81 cents each.

In November 1965 the church received electricity from Intercounty Electric Cooperative. Ken Haas hooked up the electric lights.

Pleasant Ridge Baptist Church, Weston

Reverend Albert Peter Williams founded the Pleasant Ridge Baptist Church on January 27, 1844, at a church in Weston. There were ten charter members. They decided to make the church of brick, and the bricks were made onsite by slaves. The contractor, John B. Sanford, added a balcony in the back that was used for "persons of color." The building was occupied in December 1844. It cost $2,000.

In February 1845, Reverend Robert James preached a revival at Pleasant Ridge. He was the father of outlaws Frank and Jesse James. One early member of the church was Eliza Ann Young Reynolds, widow of Governor Reynolds, who had committed suicide while in office. Another first lady of Missouri, Elnora Gabbert Park, wife of Governor Guy B. Park, had been a member. She was raised one mile north of the church.

On April 15, 1855, the church had a fire and the roof had to be repaired. After the fire, the church members white-washed the bricks until about 1900, when they were painted red as they are now. During the Civil War the roof fell in, and at this time the balcony was torn out and the cemetery door was bricked in. For several months while this work was going on, the congregation met in the chapel of the Pleasant Ridge College, which was located one-half mile south of the church. One graduate of this college was J. C. Penney, who founded the department store that bears his name.

The church voted in 1848 to establish its cemetery and lay off lots. One person who is buried here is Mrs. Mary Owens Vineyard, "Abraham Lincoln's other Mary." The Vineyard family has three letters in which Abraham Lincoln proposed marriage to Mary Owens. Three Vineyard brothers started Pleasant Ridge College. They were all members of the church.

In 1907 new pews were installed that are still in the building. In 1929 the church was wired for electricity. In 1939 services were suspended. In 1954 the church was reorganized under a church in Kansas City. It continued to hold services until the spring of 1999. The old building was put on the National Register of Historic Places on March 13, 2001, because of its age and because it had a cemetery door. This is the only church in Platte County with a cemetery door.

The Weston JC Chapter has adopted the church and plans to work on it as one of their projects. Friends of the church and members of the community are giving money for the material that will be needed.

Trinity Lutheran Church, Appleton City

When the Missouri, Kansas and Texas Railroad was built in the 1870s, little towns began to spring up along the right of way. One of these was Appleton City in southwest Missouri.

The German Evangelical Lutheran Congregation/Trinity Lutheran Church of Appleton City had its beginnings in 1870 at the Bear Creek neighborhood, five miles south and east of Germantown, the trading post and post office.

April 1874 a 20 by 30 building was erected . Served as church home about 30 yrs.

Present church was bought in 1903 Moved to sight. Paid 400.00 for church, 120.00 to move.

Services were held in the homes of the congregation, as was the custom, for lack of better facilities. One of the homes often used was that of C. Bramm, one of the first elders. The Bramm home had a large room that accommodated the worshipers who arrived in wagons. Germantown was placed on wheels and moved to what is now Montrose, Missouri. Hudson, another community close by, was also transplanted to make the town of Arlington, now Appleton City.

These changes inspired the little band of Lutherans to look for a more permanent church home. In 1874, lots in the original town of Appleton City were purchased for $150, and a twenty-by-thirty-foot building was erected for the price of $400. The lumber was hauled from Warrensburg by church members. This building served as the church home for thirty years.

The present church building was acquired in 1903 from the Trustee Land Company. It was located on Sunnyside Addition of Appleton City, which had been occupied by the Reformed Church congregation. The building was purchased for $400 and another $120 was spent on moving it. Meyers and Walker were the movers, and they used steam engines. Before the building reached its destination, something slipped and iron rods had to be installed to tie it together. That work was well done as evidenced by its excellent condition today.

Major renovation was done in 1945, when the beautiful stained-glass windows were installed. Those windows came from the Methodist Episcopal Church in the south part of town. Reverend Rohlfing built the new altar and pulpit that can be found in the church today.

Another major remodeling took place in 1962 when a basement was dug and the church was once again uplifted onto the new foundation. In 1998 a new fellowship hall was added to the east side of the church. A walkway from the church makes it accessible to all. More Sunday school rooms were added in the basement.

During its 136 years, twenty dedicated pastors have served the congregation.

1998 Dedicated 1999 New multi purpous building.

Ozark Prairie Presbyterian Church, Mount Vernon

Ozark Prairie "Brick" Presbyterian Church stands proudly and solidly on its 134-year-old native limestone foundation. The church, commonly known as the Brick Church because of its thick brick walls, rises impressively on prairie land six miles north of Mount Vernon. It was constructed from arduous work over a period of years, built to last and as a house of praise to the Lord.

The church was organized in 1854 and was first known as Lawrence Hill Church with its meetings held in private homes. Because of the unrest during the Civil War, a movement was made to move the church to a rural area and the present site was chosen. There were fifteen charter members. It is still said that the men of the church attended one of the first services fully armed.

Two acres of prairie land were provided and the foundation was completed in 1870. Bricks for the simply styled church were made on a farm three miles from the site and hauled on wagons. The pattern for the church was modeled after the Aghadowey Church in Northern Ireland. The hands of several men in the neighborhood labored to carry and lay the bricks in order to fashion walls seventeen inches thick.

After much effort, the landmark church was completed in 1872 at a cost of $6,000 and the name was changed to Ozark Prairie. In subsequent yeas a narthex, balcony, and classrooms were added. In recent years a fellowship hall designed to blend in with the original structure was constructed.

The church has survived a tornado, strong winds and lightning in addition to economic depressions and changing times. Ozark Electric Cooperative brought electricity to the Brick Church in 1939, replacing a pressure gasoline lighting plant. A gas heating unit was installed in 1950, a replacement for two large, black wood-burning stoves, whose vent pipes reached to the high ceiling and extended out the back of the building. Air conditioning, a well, a bathroom, and kitchen were added in later years, along with an electric organ that was added during the congregation's one-hundredth year.

The church has been well maintained and presents a dignified and impressive appearance. The original pews and pulpit, handcrafted from native rough walnut timber that is polished to a warm patina, are still used. Legend has it the wood came from an enormous tree.

In the early years of the church when travel was difficult, the preacher only came two Sundays a month and they often stayed at the home of a church elder. Services the rest of the month were conducted by one of the elders.

Christmas programs at "The Brick" are a memorable tradition. A large cedar tree is brought inside and the custom in earlier years was to decorate it with lighted candles, strung popcorn, and homemade decorations. Today the tree is decorated with lights and other bright decorations. The program is presented by the children and consists of speeches, songs, and a pageant. Santa arrives and gift socks filled with oranges and candy await everyone. One Yule season, the selected tree was so large a mule was pressed into service to pull it into the church.

Today's members are proud of the history and strength of this rural church, especially in an era when country churches have so fast disappeared from the scene.

Coal Hill Community of Christ Church, El Dorado Springs

On September 10, 1882, a branch of the Community of Christ Church was organized near the town of Clintonville in Cedar County, Missouri. Members who moved here had been meeting in homes and schools. In 1882, the church had grown so much it was decided to build a church building. It was called Coal Hill Chapel because it was close to Coal Hill School and Coal Hill Cemetery. The name Coal Hill comes from the large vein of coal and surrounding strip mines from which many of the landowners dug coal to help meet living expenses and heat their homes.

Abner Lloyd donated land for the building to stand upon. During 1894 and 1895, it was noted there were 219 recorded members. Horse and buggy was the only means of travel.

Bucklin Christian Church, Bucklin

The Bucklin Christian Church serves a small congregation of about 125 active members. Brother James Webb serves as its current pastor and spiritual leader. This is a praying congregation that uses the Bible for a guide to living.

There was a congregation of Disciples of Christ in Bucklin as early as 1867. The current building was built by J. A. Richardson, architect, and dedicated by George Snively on May 14, 1911. Behind the main building is an annex housing the Sunday school rooms.

One of the church's most important traditions is the Sunrise Service held every Easter morning. The sunshine and dawn coming through the beautiful stained-glass windows in front of the church is glorious and inspirational to all. It is a homecoming time for many families. After the early service, everyone gathers in the dining room for a big breakfast. It doesn't matter how long or far you've been gone. Those who attend know they are home on Easter morning.

Mt. Tabor Baptist Church, Atlanta

This church was organized on December 4, 1840. The first church was built of hewn logs in 1848 and was located twenty-five or thirty feet south of the entrance gate to the present cemetery. The original members were Mr. and Mrs. J. L. Arthur, Mr. and Mrs. Logan Thompson, and Mr. and Mrs. John Silvers.

Mt. Tabor furnished the nucleus around which the association was formed. The constitution and articles of faith of the old Cumberland River Association of Kentucky were adopted, and the association took the name of Mt. Tabor Association of United Baptists. It became Macon Baptist Association in 1866.

After the log church's chinking began to fall out, a new church was built. In 1867 a brick building was built under the direction of Reverend James Moody, an early settler from Kentucky. The brick was made on Bailey's Branch, less than a quarter mile from the site. This church building was located across the road from the present site. It cost $1,700. It contained a number of large columns and homemade seats. It was torn down in 1898, when the building that stands today was built. The day work started on the present church, twenty-five men with their teams hauled rock from west of Tenmile for the foundation.

Several improvements have been made over the years, including an addition of Sunday school rooms and a bathroom along with a basement and modern kitchen. The pulpit was donated by Reverend Vernon Miles in memory of his parents. The Travis family donated the piano in memory of Mrs. Donald Travis. Mr. and Mrs. Phillip Brockman gave the organ in memory of their parents.

In 1999 the church received extensive damage from a tornado. At this time all the windows were replaced, new carpet laid, and pews refinished. The pews are original to 1898.

Mt. Zion Methodist Church, Redman

Mt. Zion Church was first organized in 1869 at the Iowa Schoolhouse about 2.5 miles northwest of the present site. Ten years later the Mount Zion Episcopal Church was built at the present location on land received from M. D. and Sarah Huston. A Mr. Shed was the carpenter with men in the neighborhood helping. On July 1, 1906, it was rededicated after remodeling, adding the present rostrum and Sunday school room.

The old church faced south and also had a door in the north. The bell tower is thought to have been removed in the early 1930s after leaking made it difficult to repair. The full basement was added in 1957 and provides a lovely place for gatherings.

Many a memory can be relived as families gather from all over for the Easter Sunrise Service, the homemade ice cream socials, basket dinners or the Annual Lord's Acre Sale, which began in 1951 and is held the last Saturday in October. The very special Christmas Eve Program is held each year unless snow blocks the roads. Records show it was cancelled due to muddy roads in 1941 and because of snowdrifts in 1982.

The current pastor is "Preacher Lady" Sheila Swafford, who is shared with sister churches Atlanta and La Plata United Methodist. She not only takes care of the church family but also helps out in community mission projects and is a member of the Grandma Cooks who provide meals for youth work camps throughout the Midwest.

The door here is always open for you to come and worship.

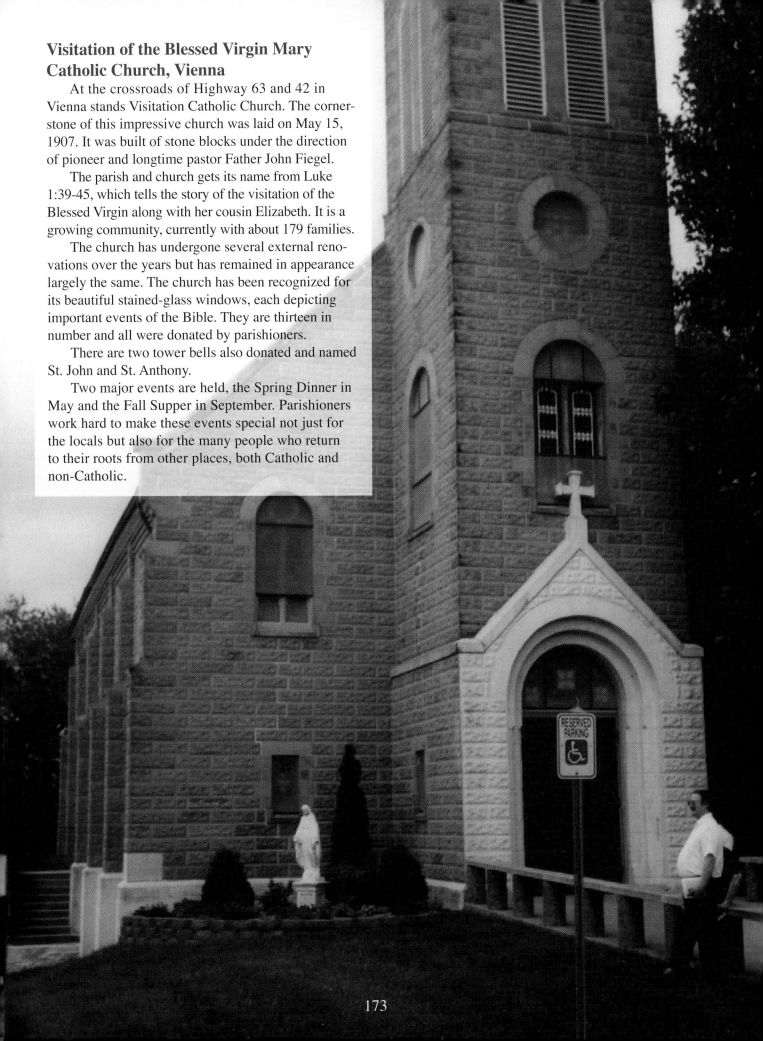

Visitation of the Blessed Virgin Mary Catholic Church, Vienna

At the crossroads of Highway 63 and 42 in Vienna stands Visitation Catholic Church. The cornerstone of this impressive church was laid on May 15, 1907. It was built of stone blocks under the direction of pioneer and longtime pastor Father John Fiegel.

The parish and church gets its name from Luke 1:39-45, which tells the story of the visitation of the Blessed Virgin along with her cousin Elizabeth. It is a growing community, currently with about 179 families.

The church has undergone several external renovations over the years but has remained in appearance largely the same. The church has been recognized for its beautiful stained-glass windows, each depicting important events of the Bible. They are thirteen in number and all were donated by parishioners.

There are two tower bells also donated and named St. John and St. Anthony.

Two major events are held, the Spring Dinner in May and the Fall Supper in September. Parishioners work hard to make these events special not just for the locals but also for the many people who return to their roots from other places, both Catholic and non-Catholic.

INDEX

Background photo: St. John L and R Church of Christ, Mount Hope

175

ABOUT THE AUTHOR

Linda C. Kerns was raised in church from the time she was two and came to a saving knowledge of Christ at the age of five. She is the daughter of a bi-vocational Baptist pastor/construction worker and has been intrigued with religion and architecture since childhood. She is the middle child of three and the only girl. Her ambition to write was encouraged by her entire family but was often inspired by her mother who has always had a talent for writing. Linda believes that her writing is a gift from God and feels that it is a blessing to have.

She is an English major with a desire to teach college English. She has participated in two different tutoring programs: AmeriCorps, tutoring second and third graders in the Republic school system, and working as a peer tutor in the writing center on the Ozark Technical Community College Campus. Through her work with AmeriCorps, she was introduced to President Bill Clinton and was also awarded the Missouri Lieutenant Governor's Service Award.

She has lived in several states including Alaska, where she worked as a floral designer and clerk in a sewing supply/tourist business. It was here that she had the distinct privilege of meeting President Ronald Reagan and Nancy Reagan shortly after he left office as they cruised the islands of Alaska. She also enjoyed the primitive living and unspoiled outdoors of the frontier state.

Linda currently lives outside of Jefferson City with her friend Pam and their two dogs Ziggy and Punk. She works as a legislative assistant for a representative in the Missouri State Capitol. She attends Harvest Time Ministries in Holts Summit. Her life verses are John 16:33 and 1st Peter 5:7. She enjoys being outdoors, camping, bicycling, and writing. This is her first book. She has previously had two poems published.

St. Marcus German Evangelical Church,
Near Hermann

United Methodist Church, Schell City